# Don't Wait, Create!

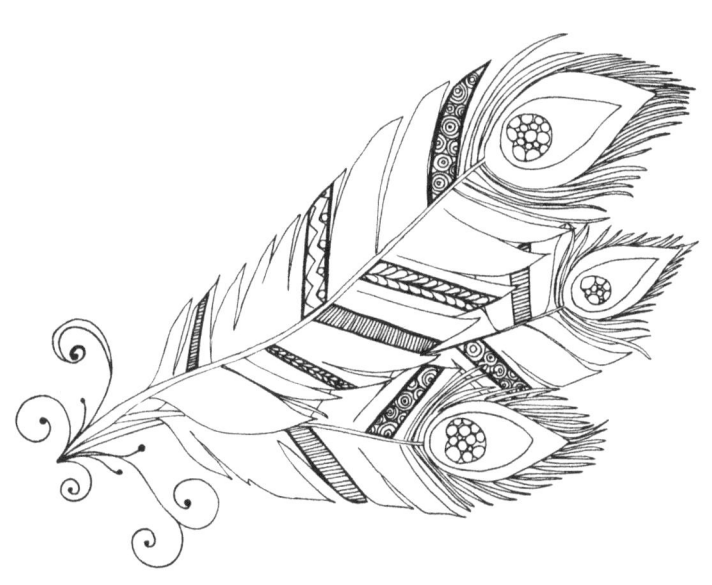

## Illistrations and Concept by Wendy Story

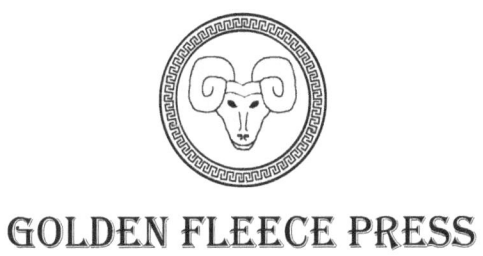

GOLDEN FLEECE PRESS

For permission requests, write to the publisher, addressed "Attention: Permissions Coordinator," at the address below.
Golden Fleece Press
PO Box 1464,
Centreville, VA 20122
www.goldenfleecepress.com

Special discounts are available on quantity purchases by corporations, associations, and others. For details, contact the publisher at the address above. U.S. trade bookstores and wholesalers please contact Ingram Content Group at customerservice@ingramcontent.com or by telephone at 800.973.8000(option 3).

Print ISBN 13: 978-1-942195-42-9

Printed in the United States of America

First Edition

10 9 8 7 6 5 4 3 2 1

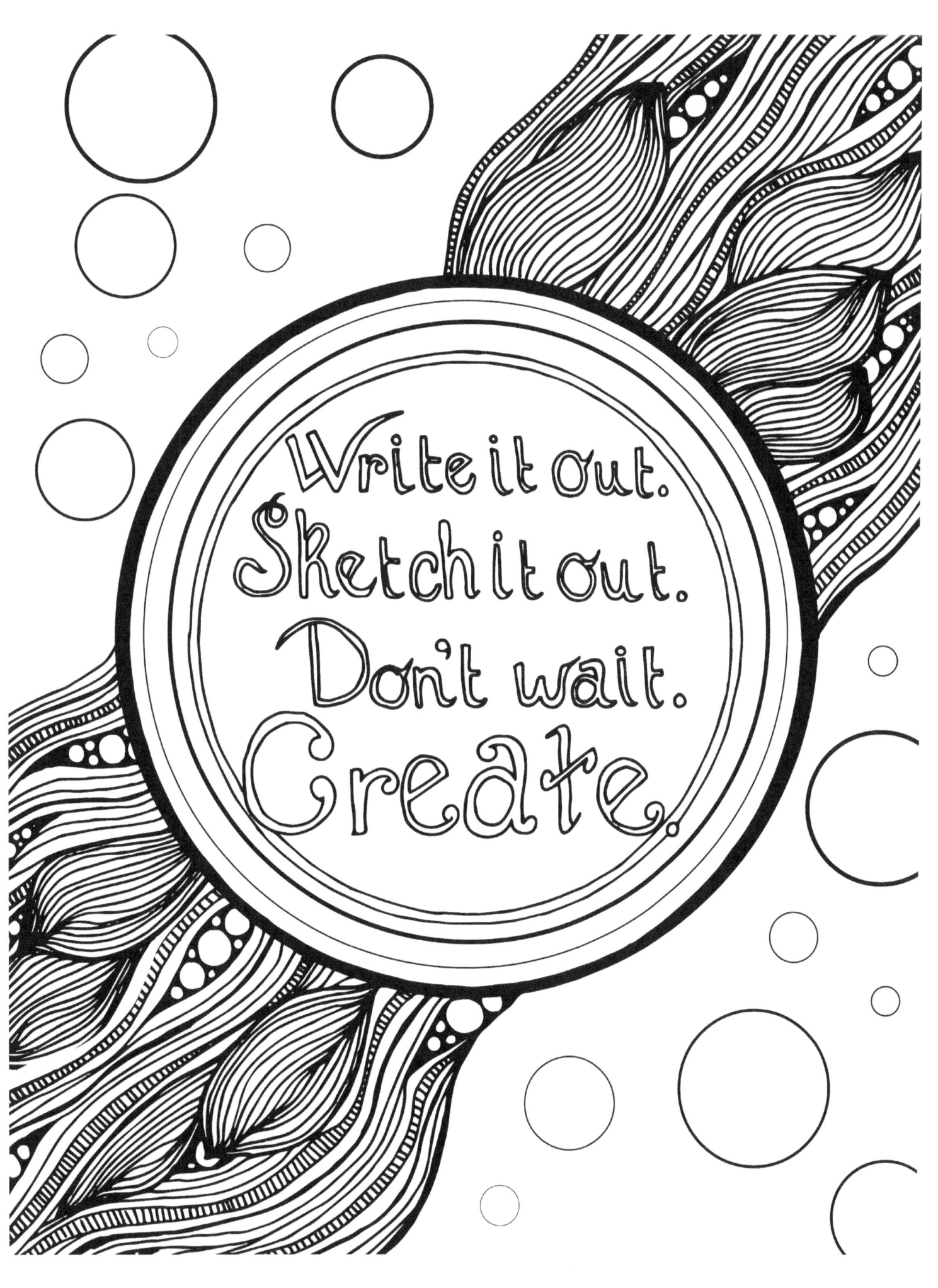

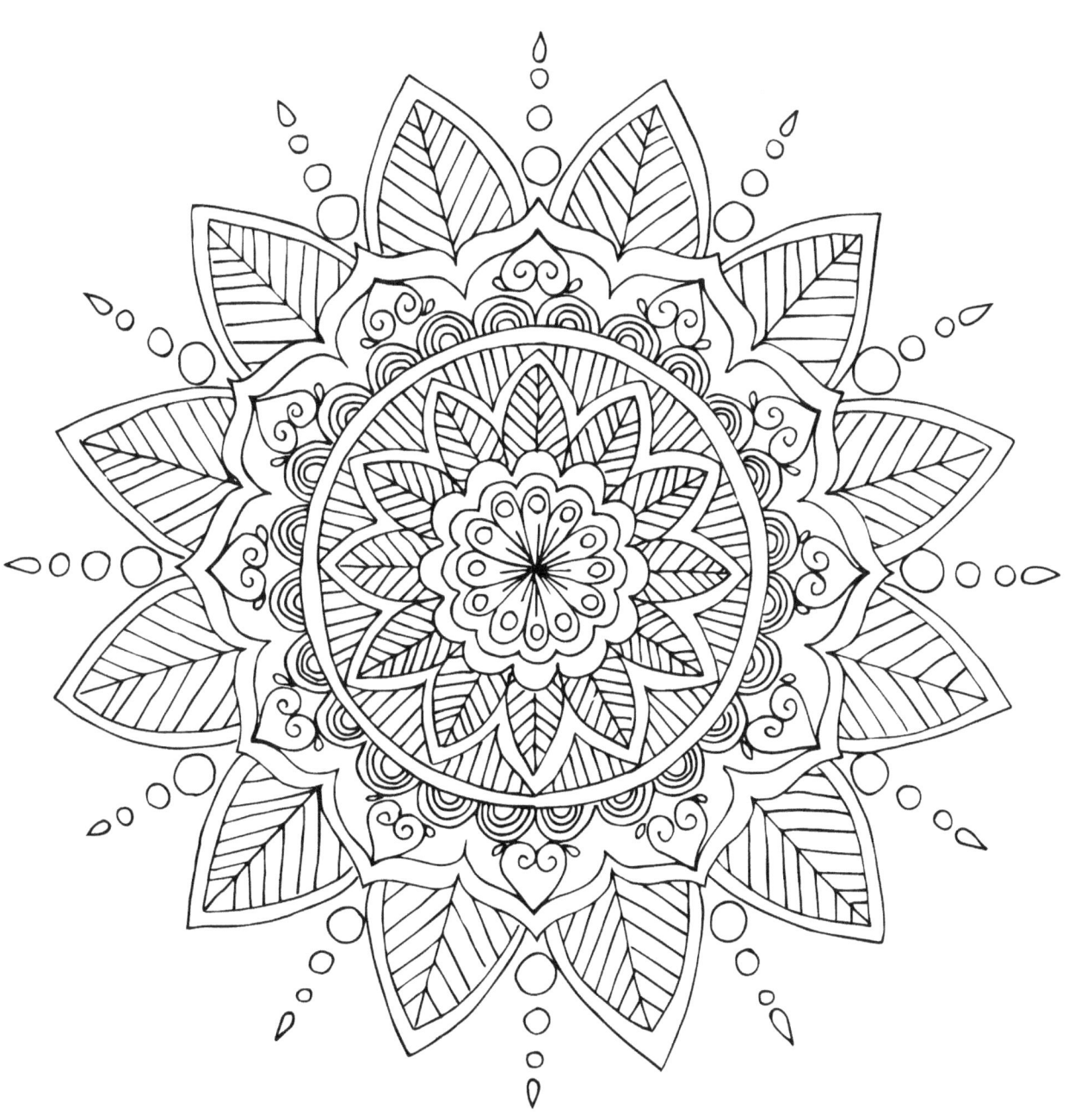

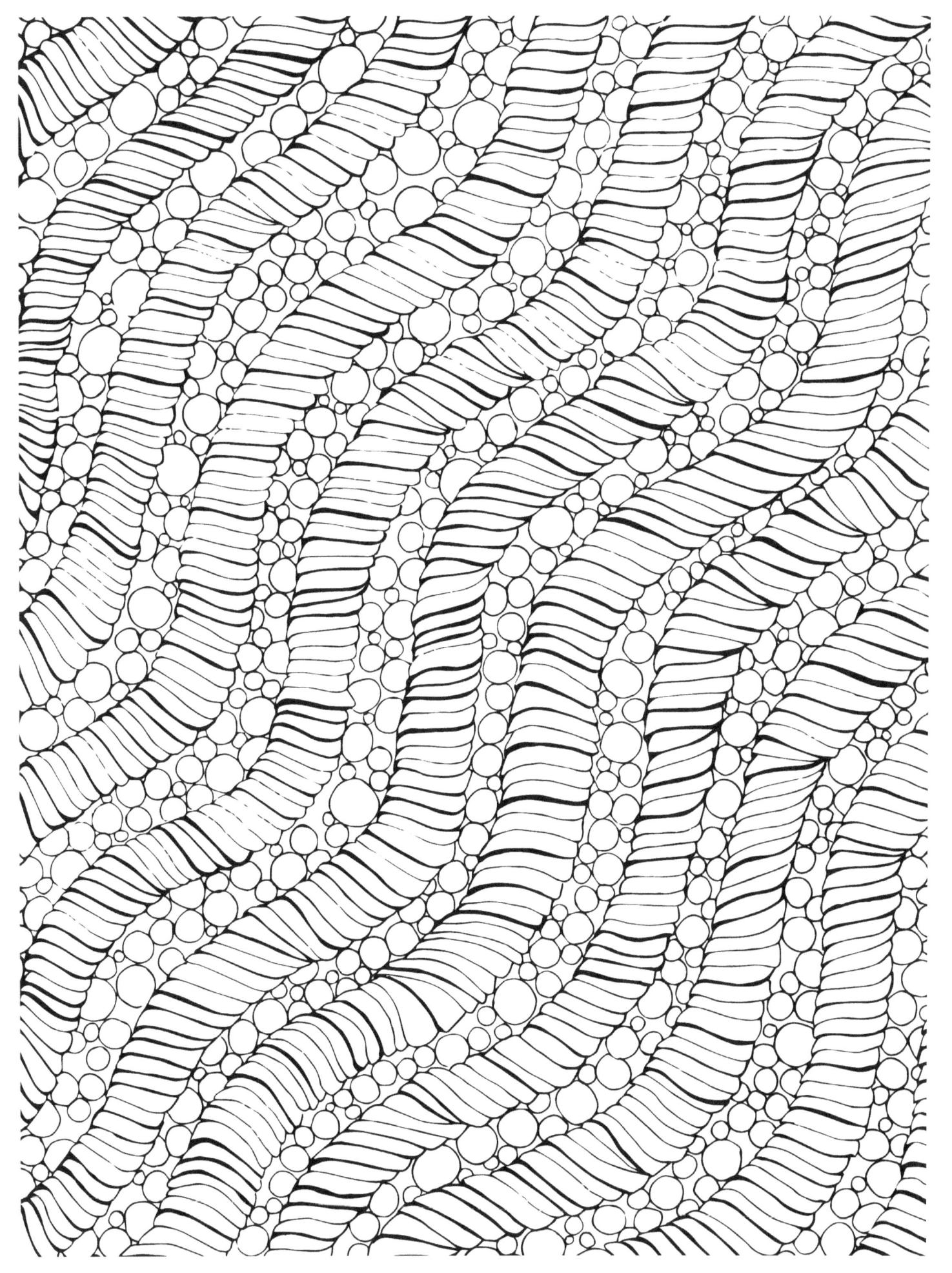

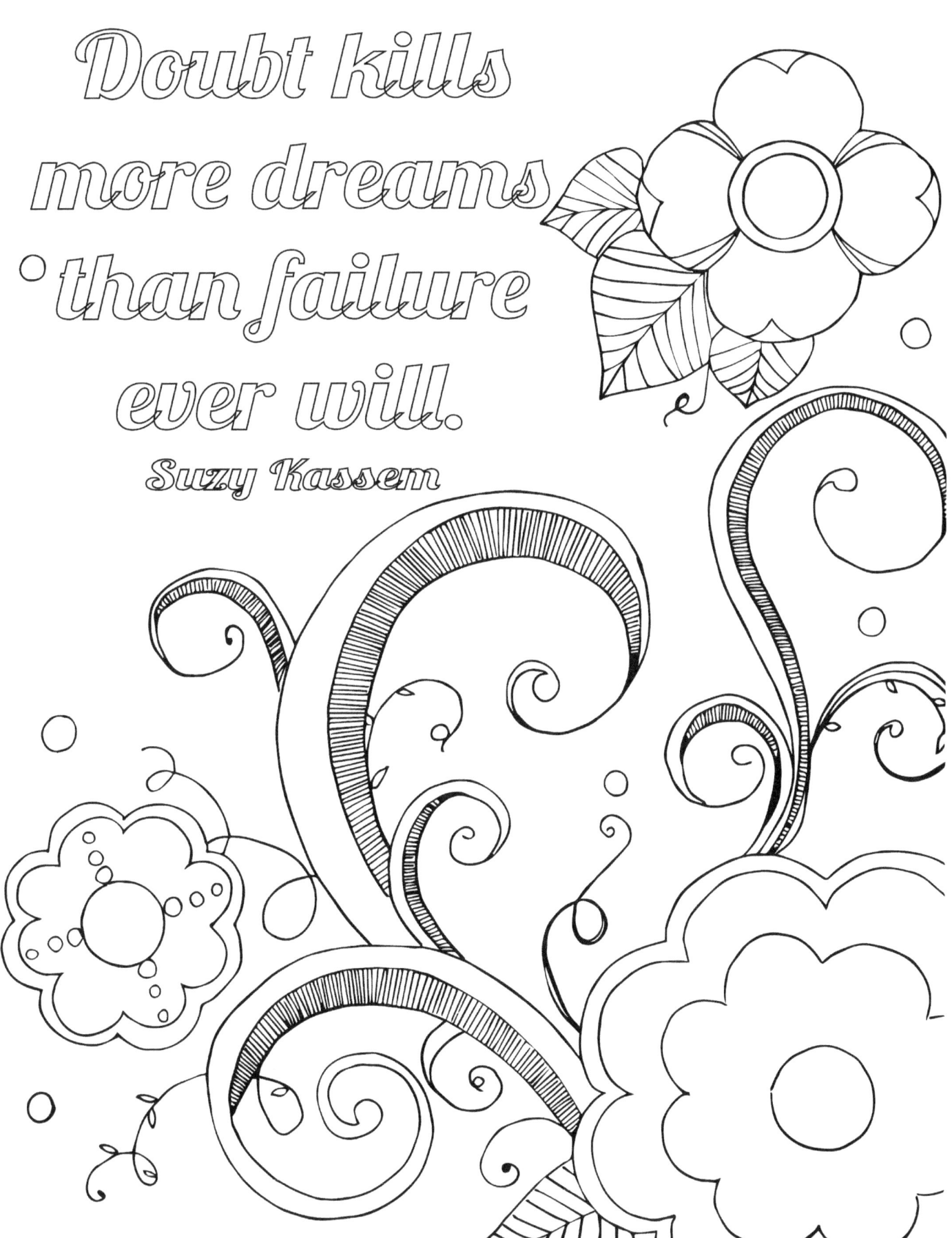

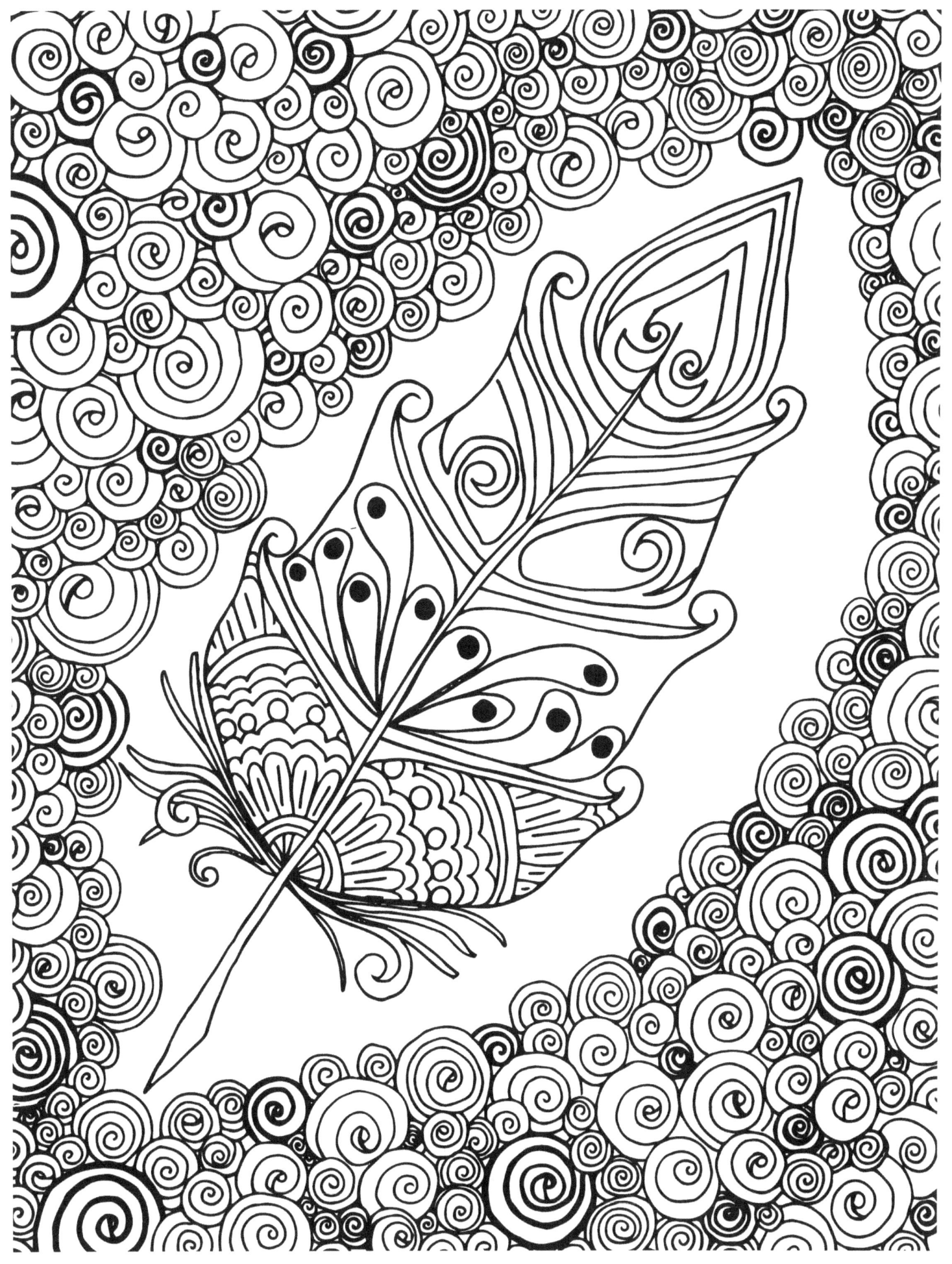

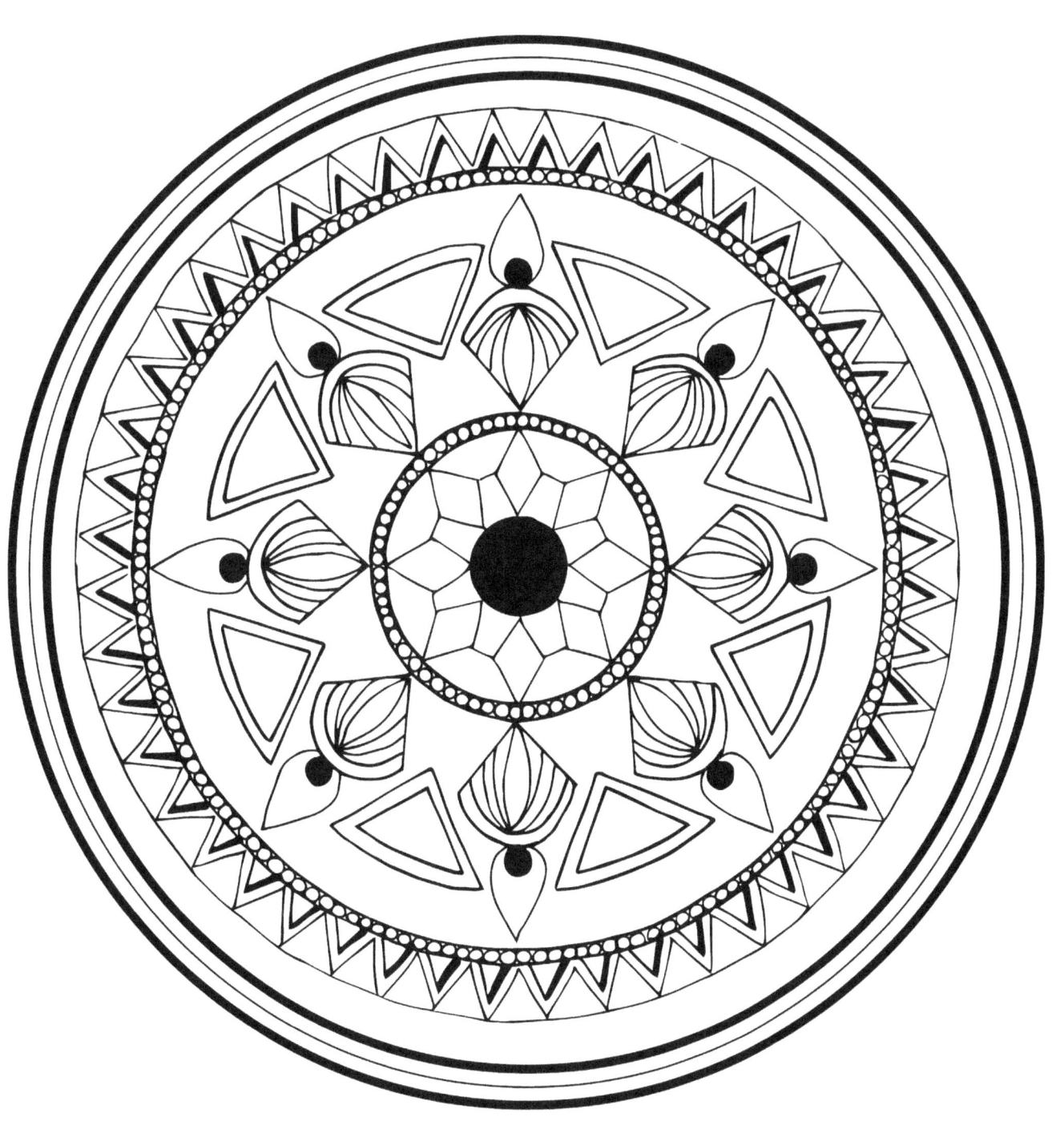

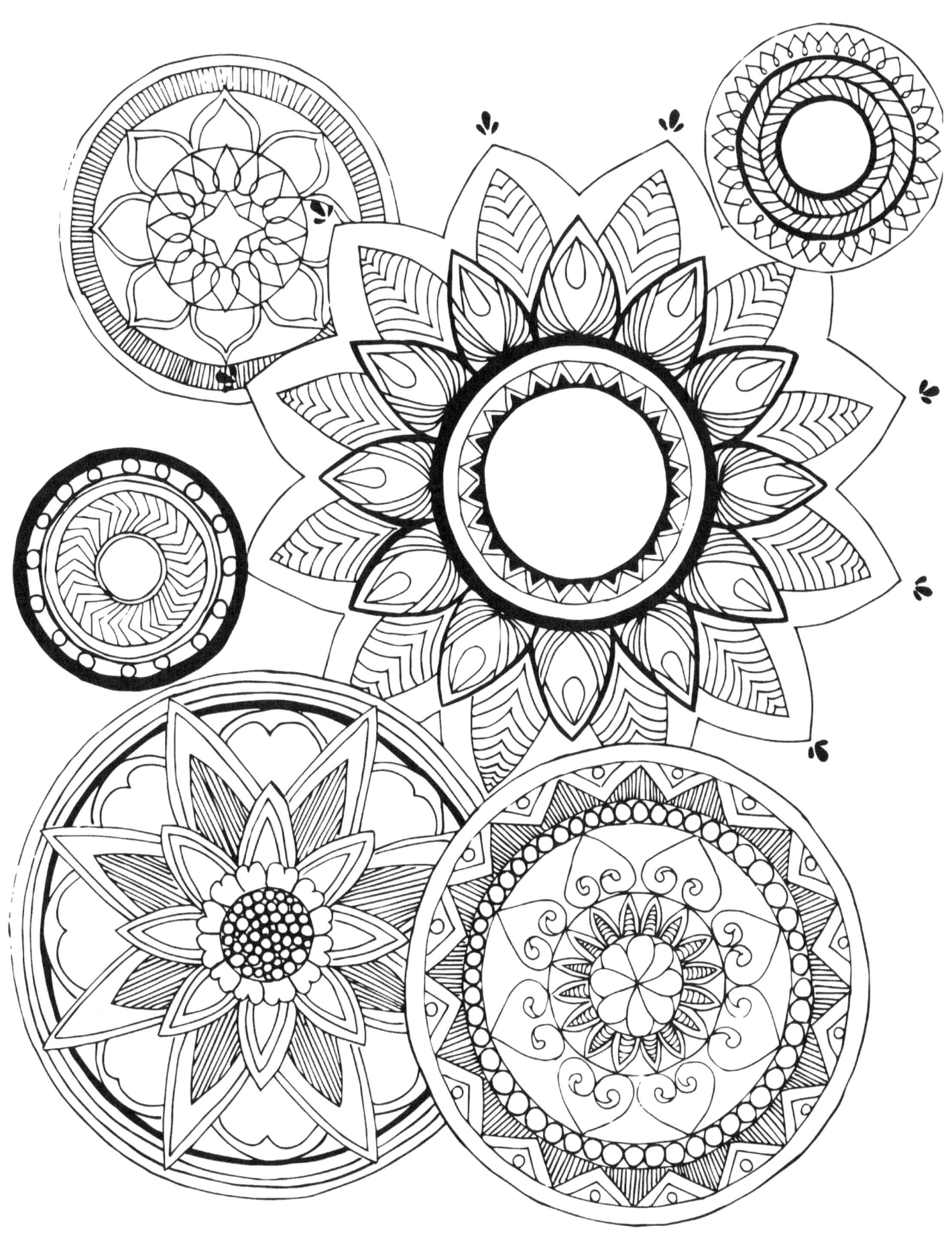

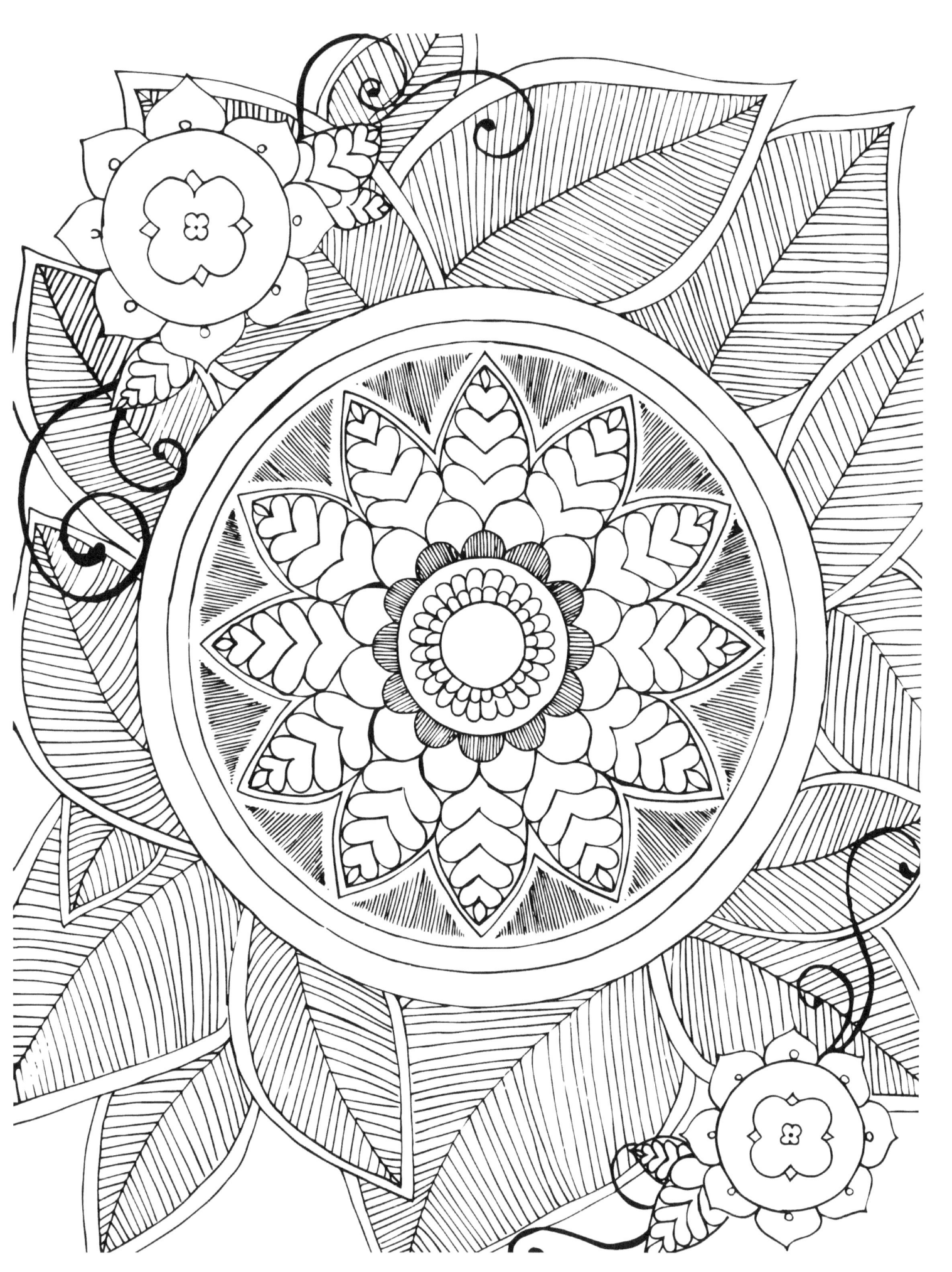

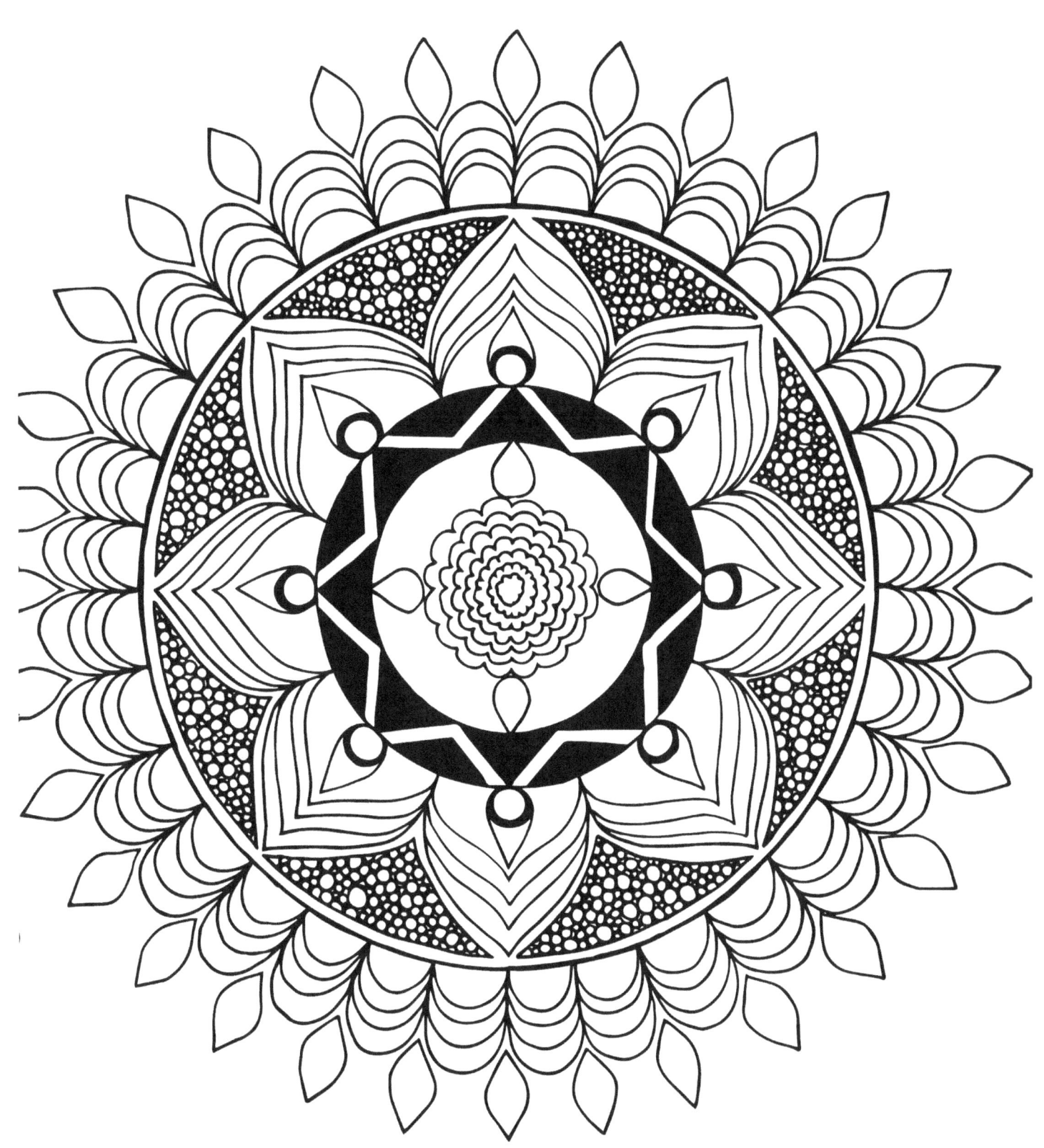

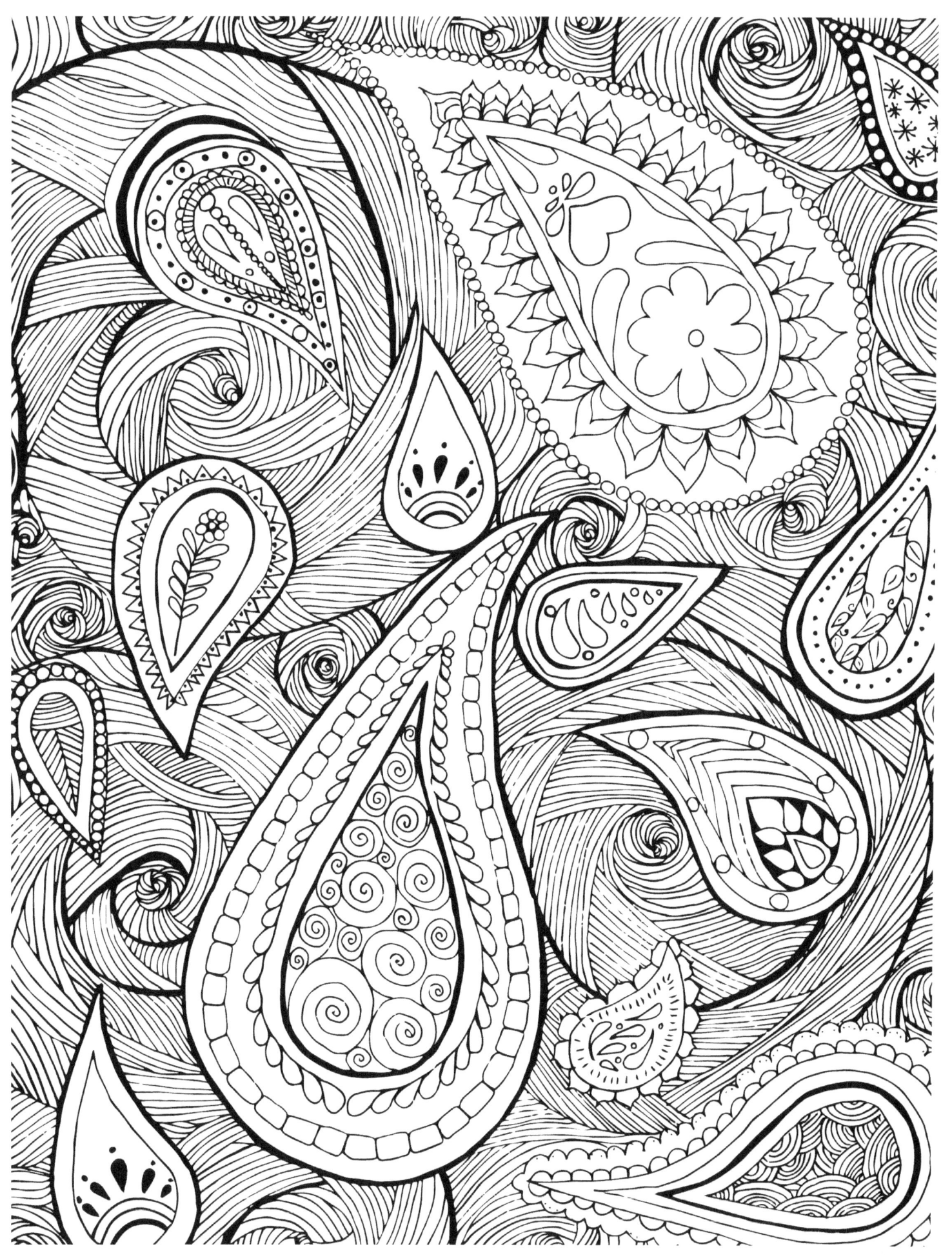

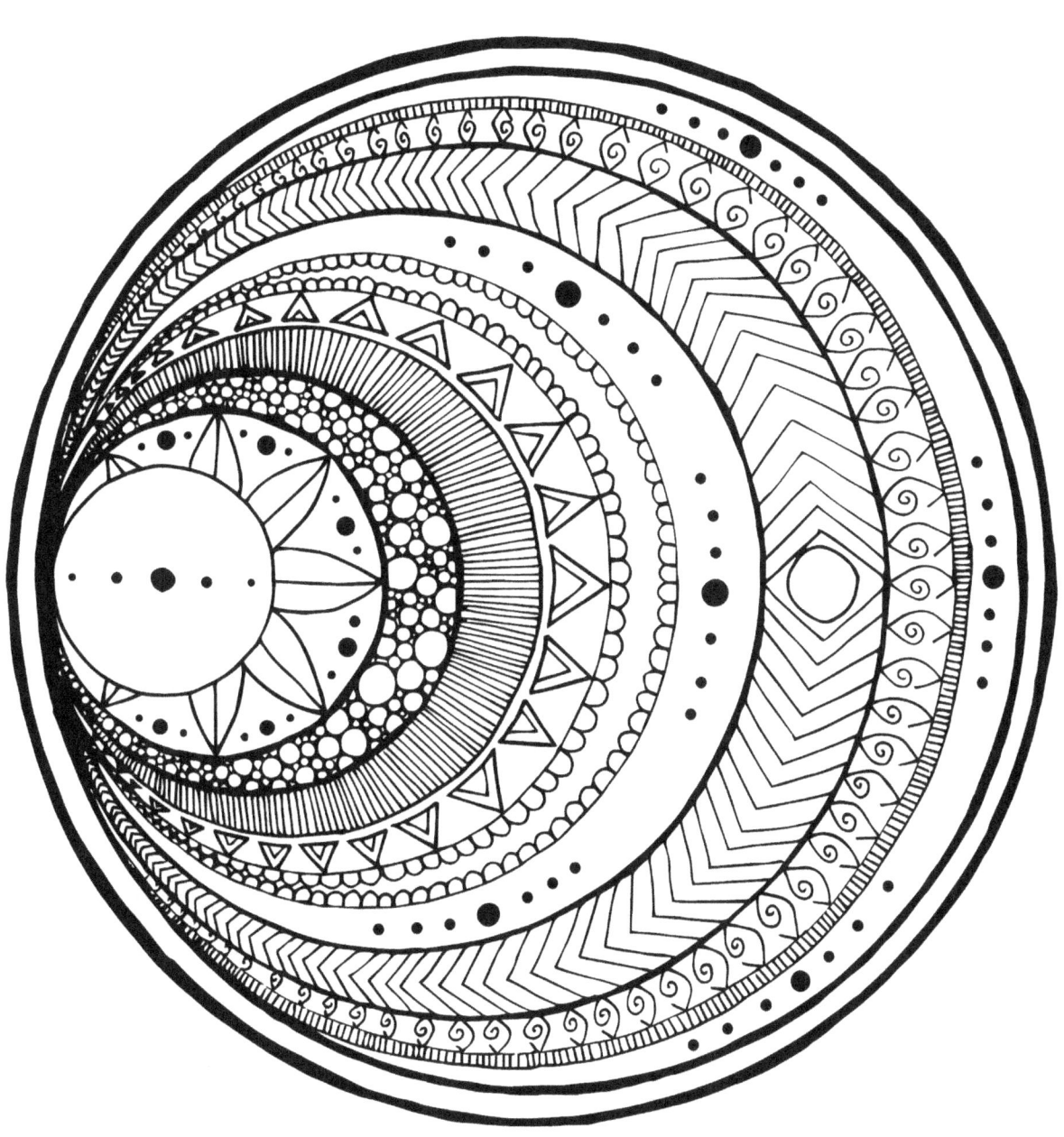

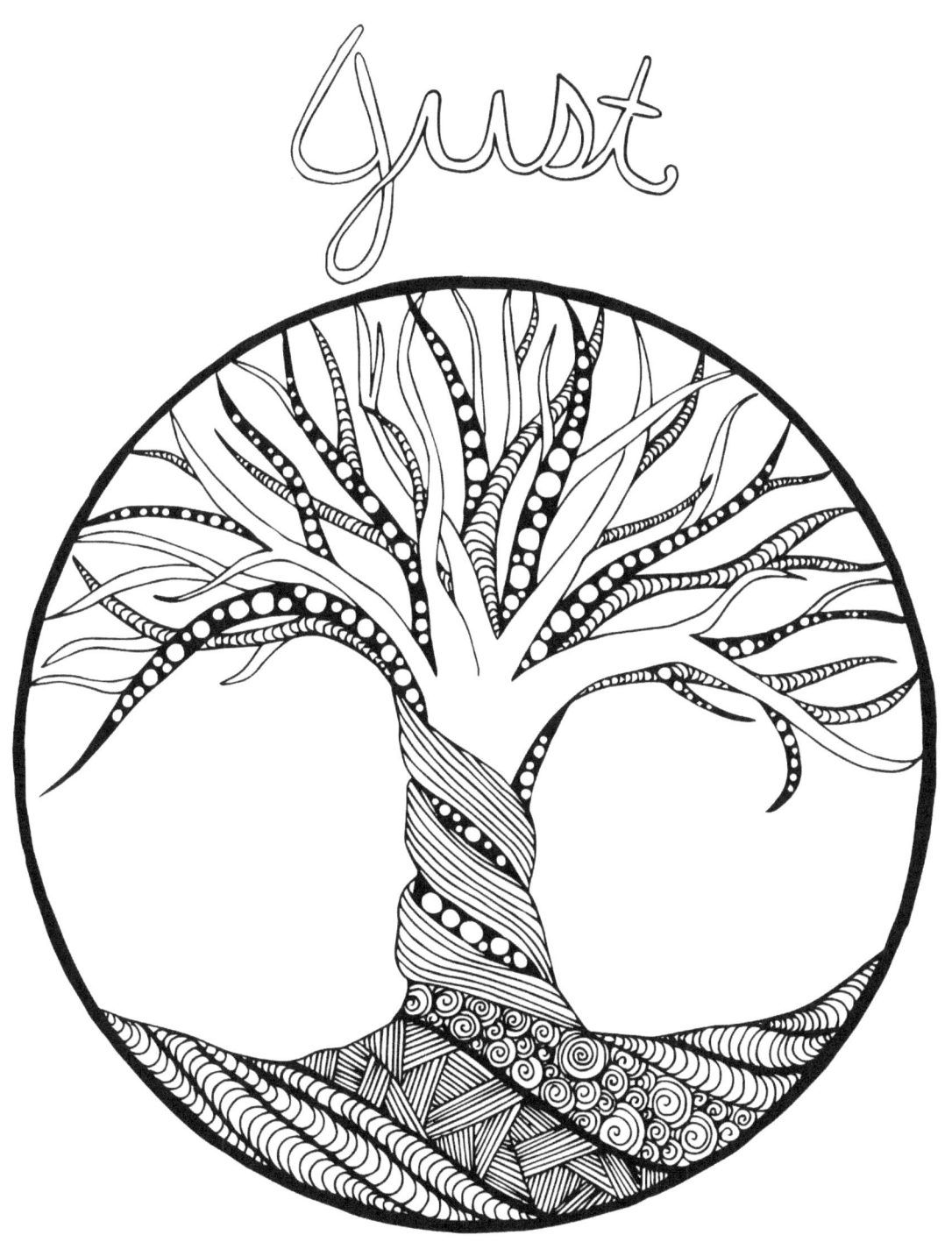

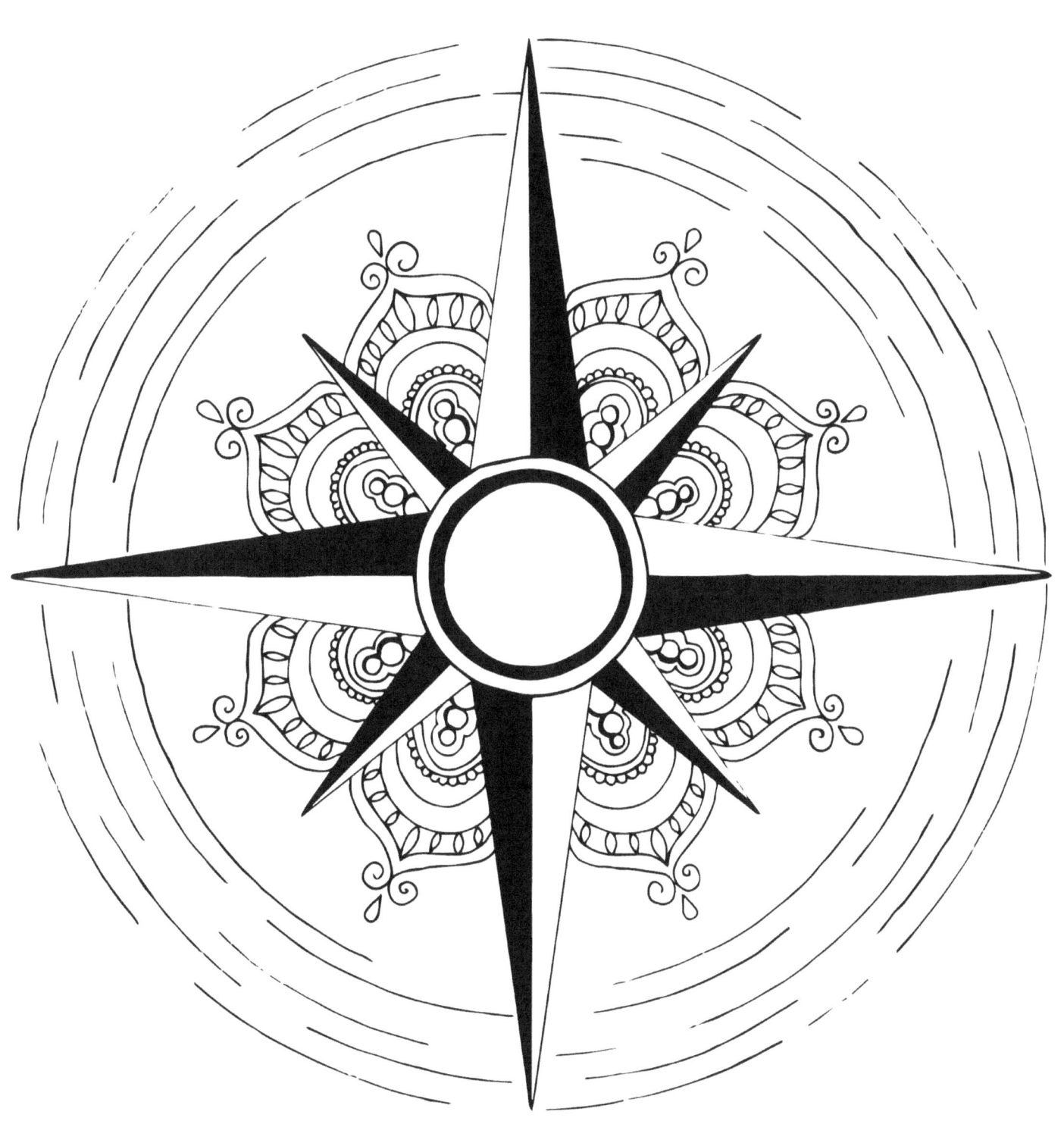

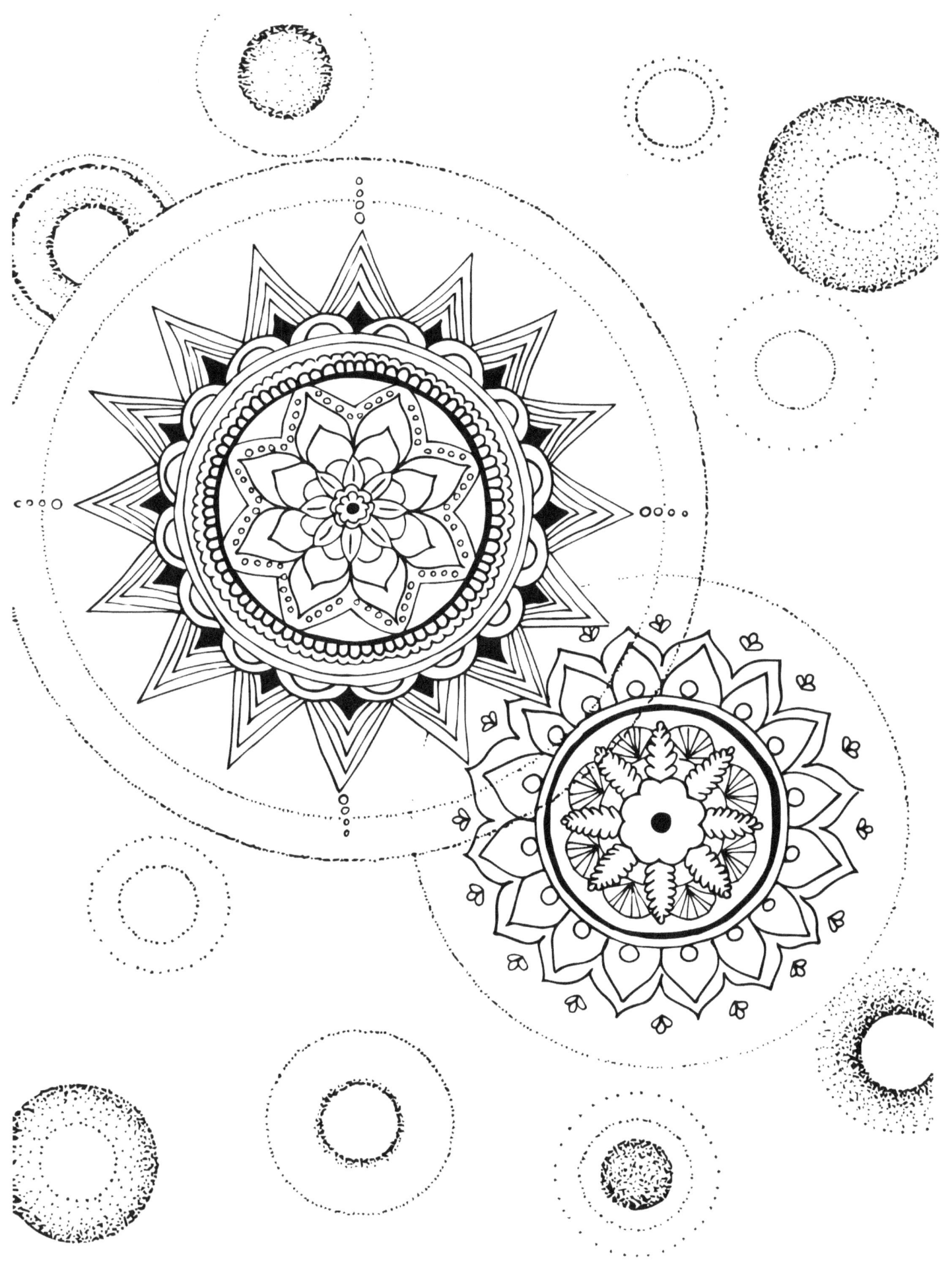

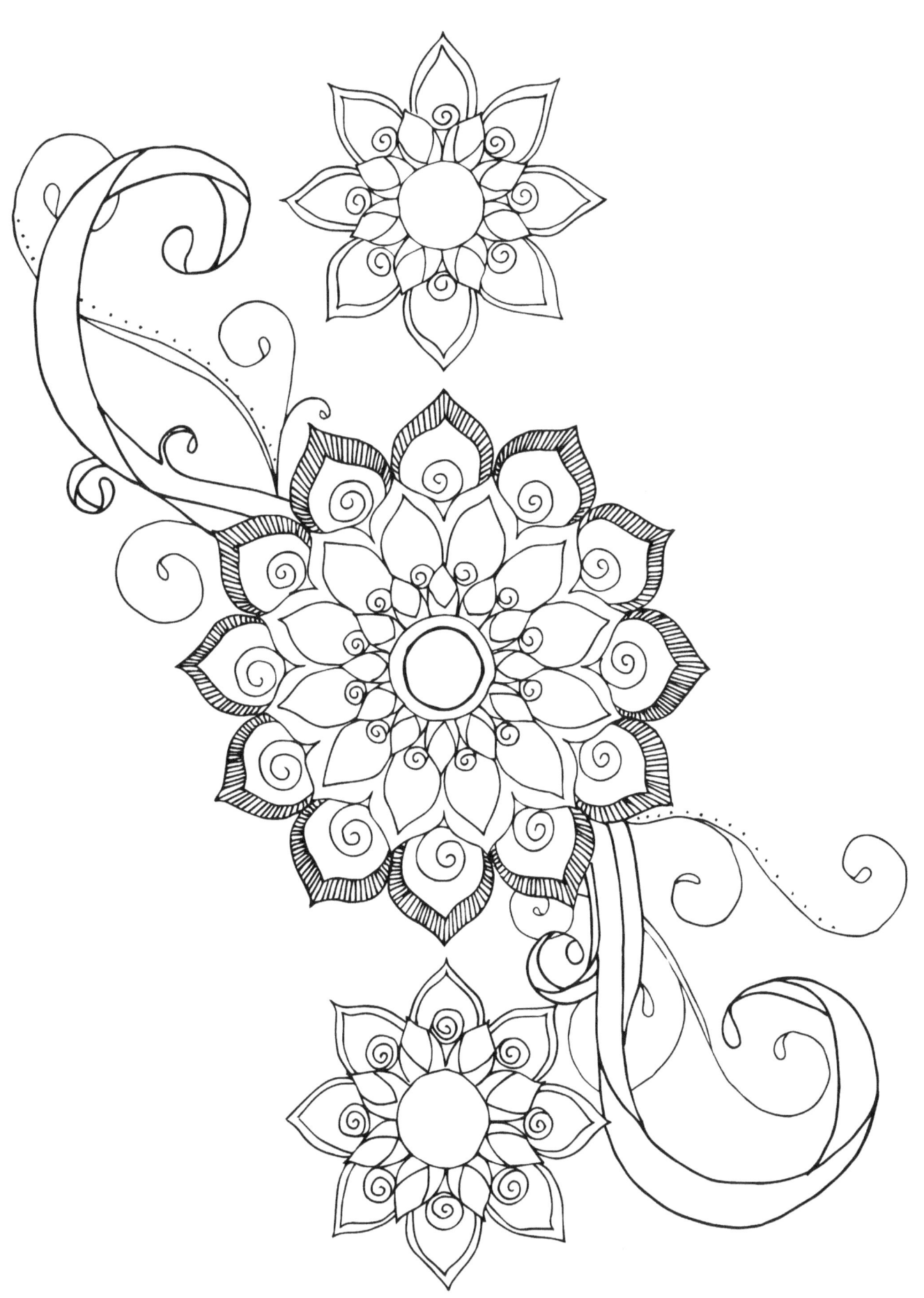

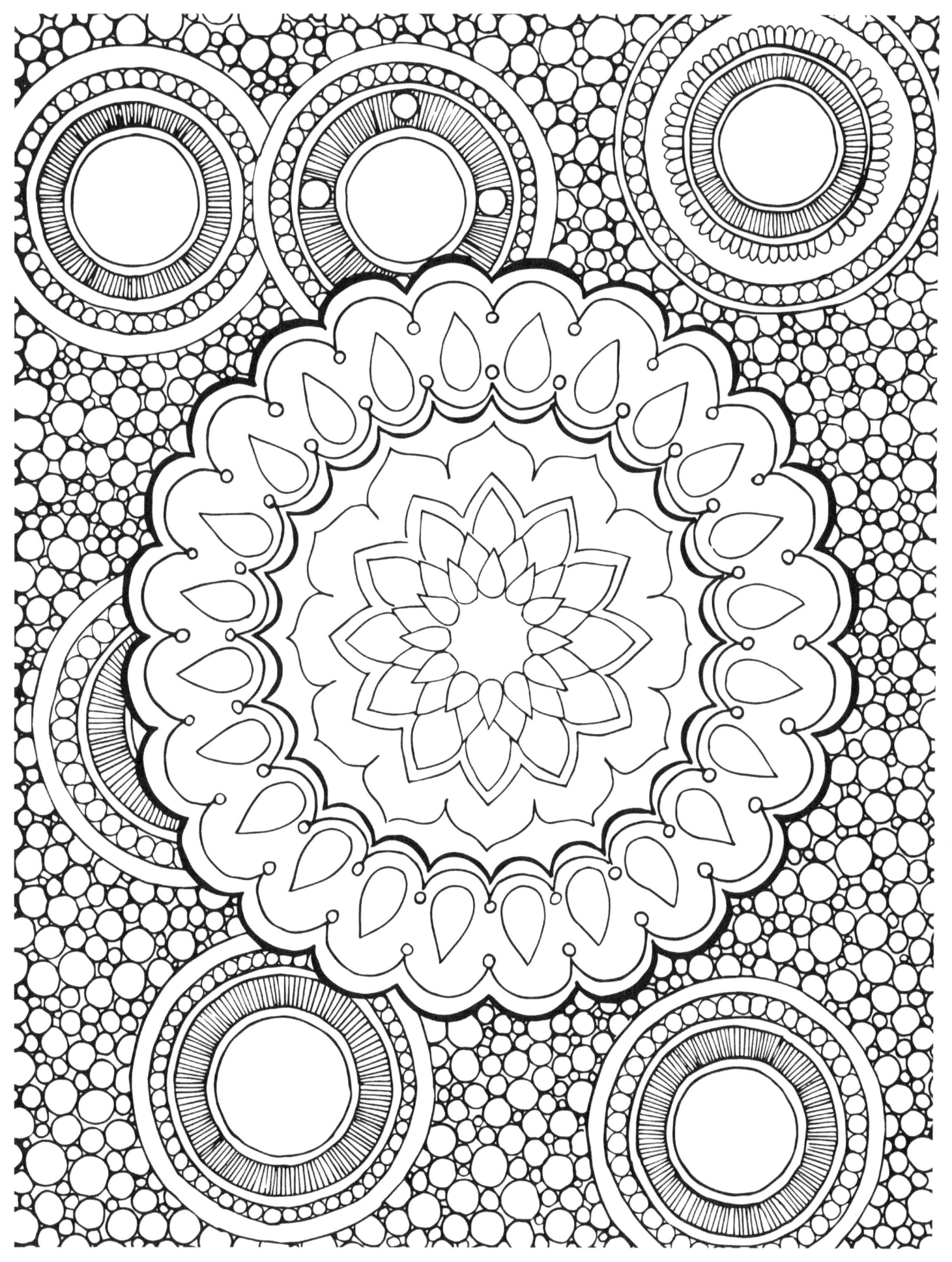

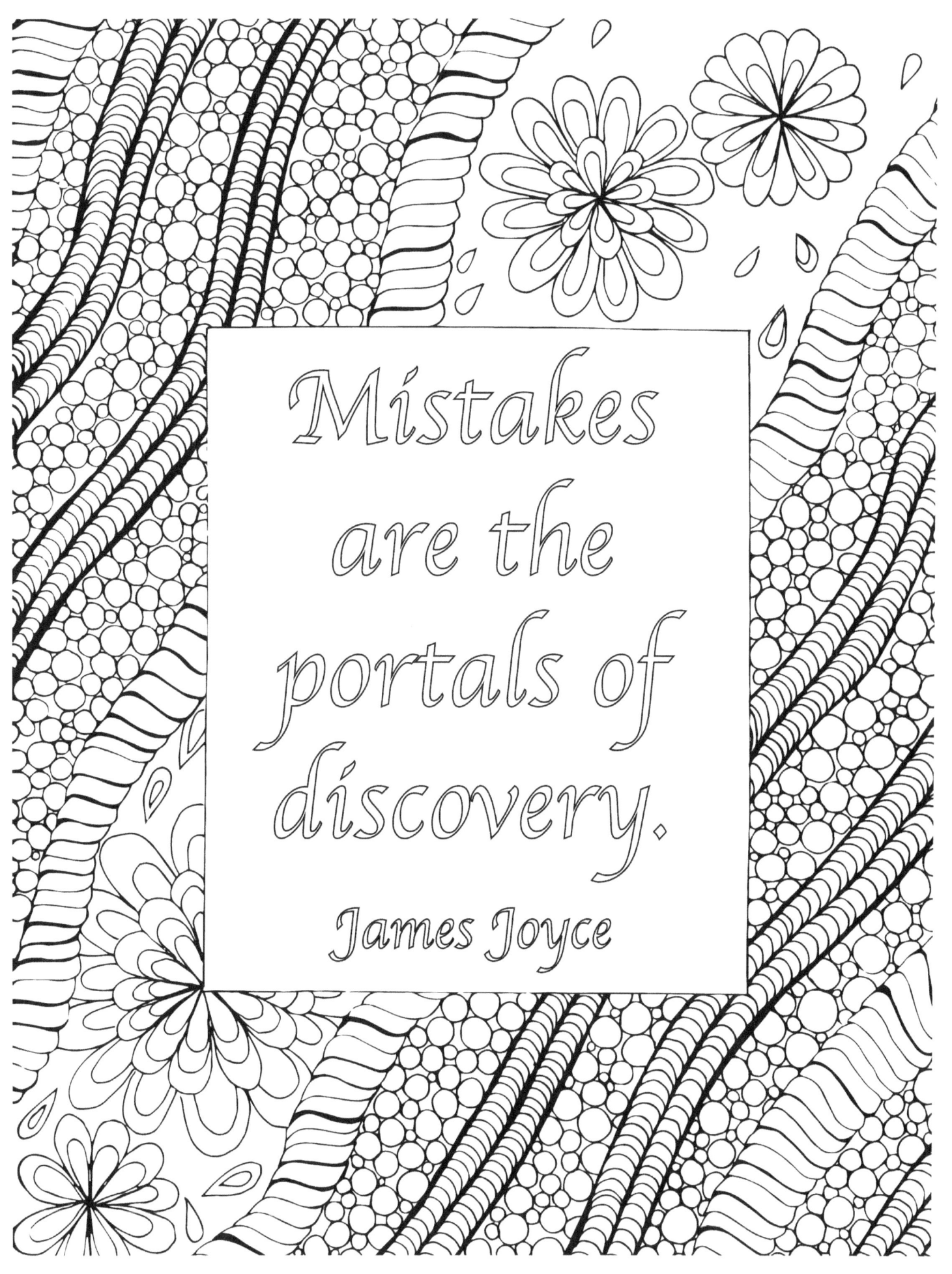

Mistakes are the portals of discovery.

James Joyce

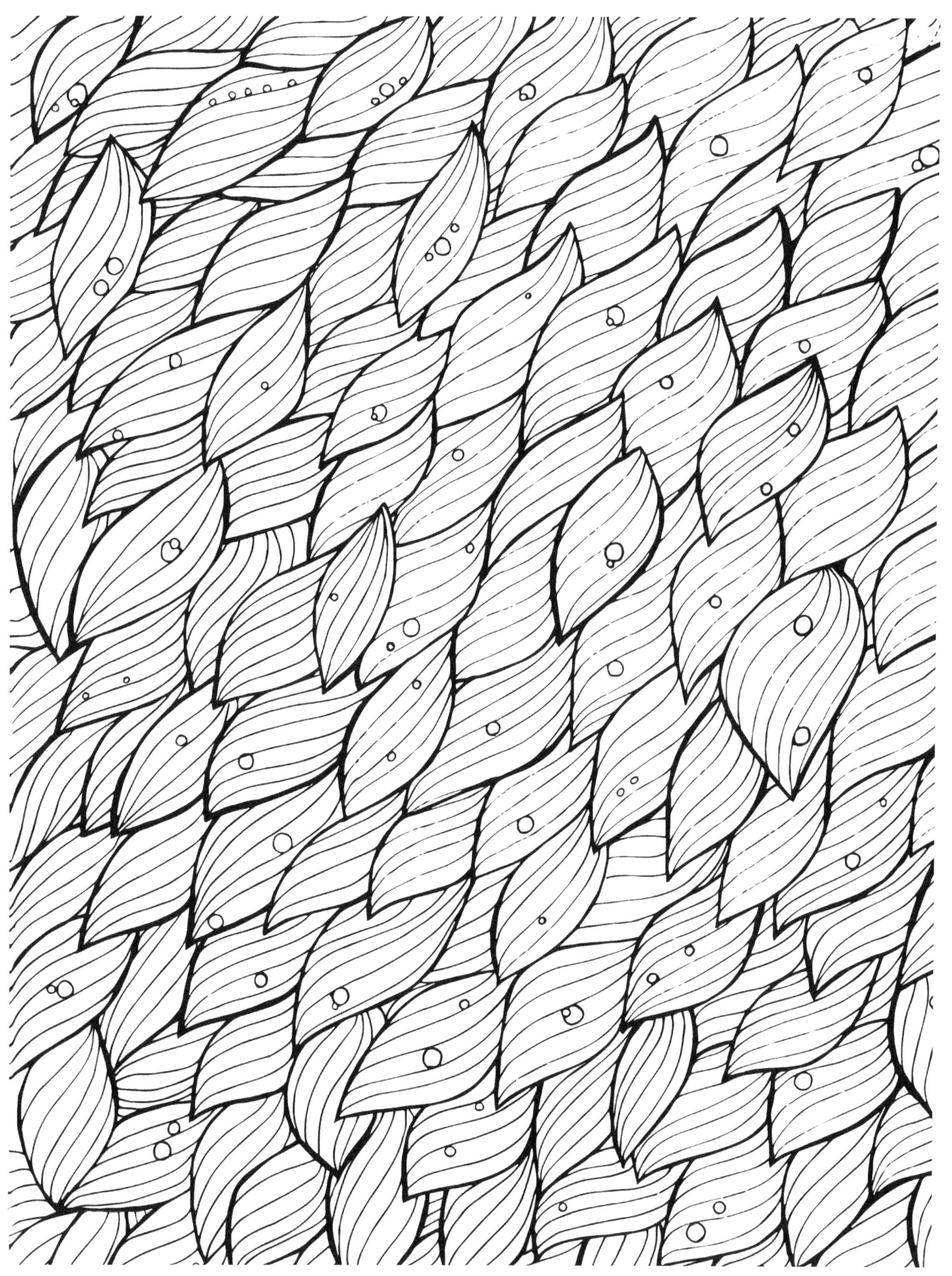

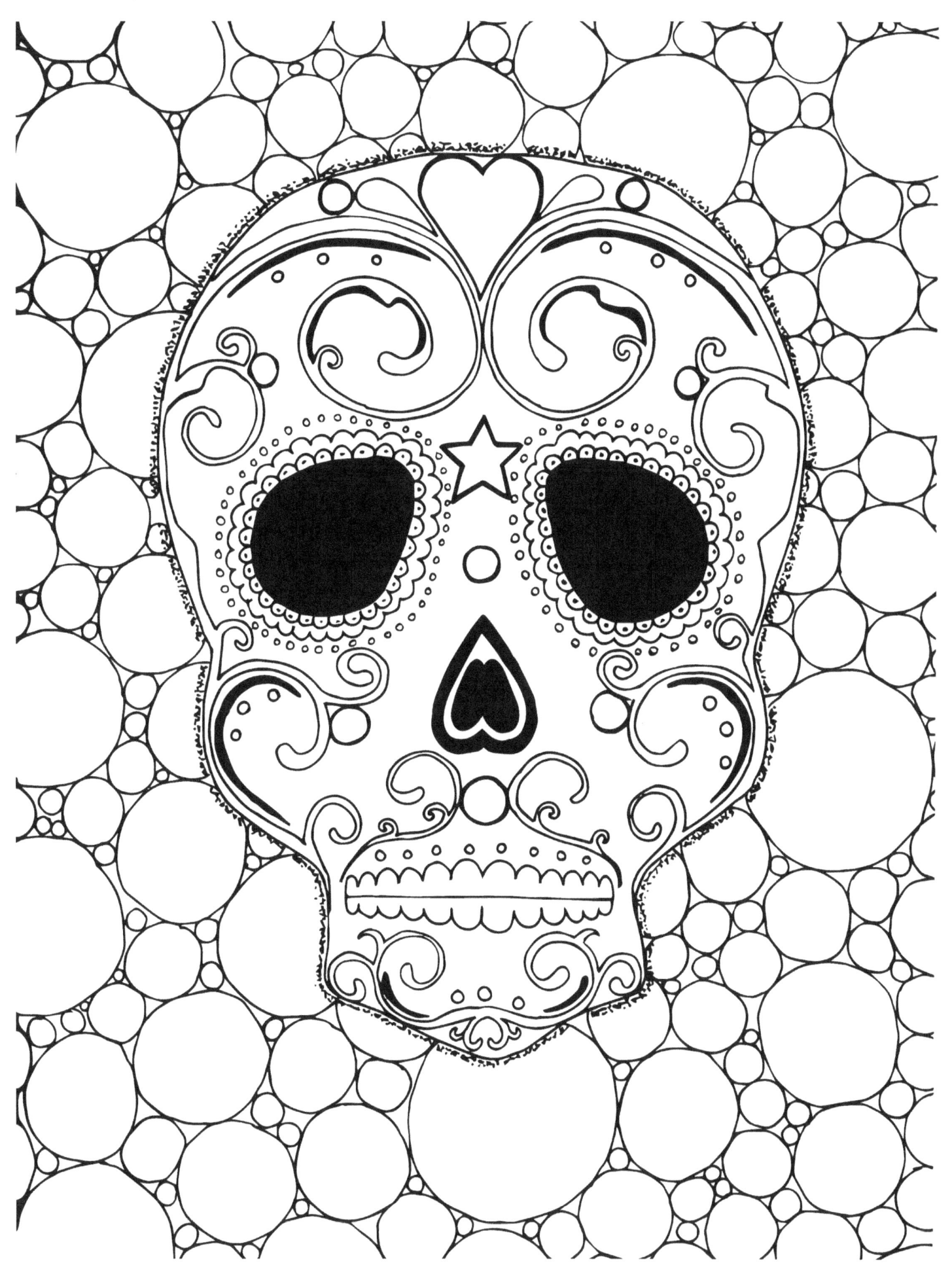

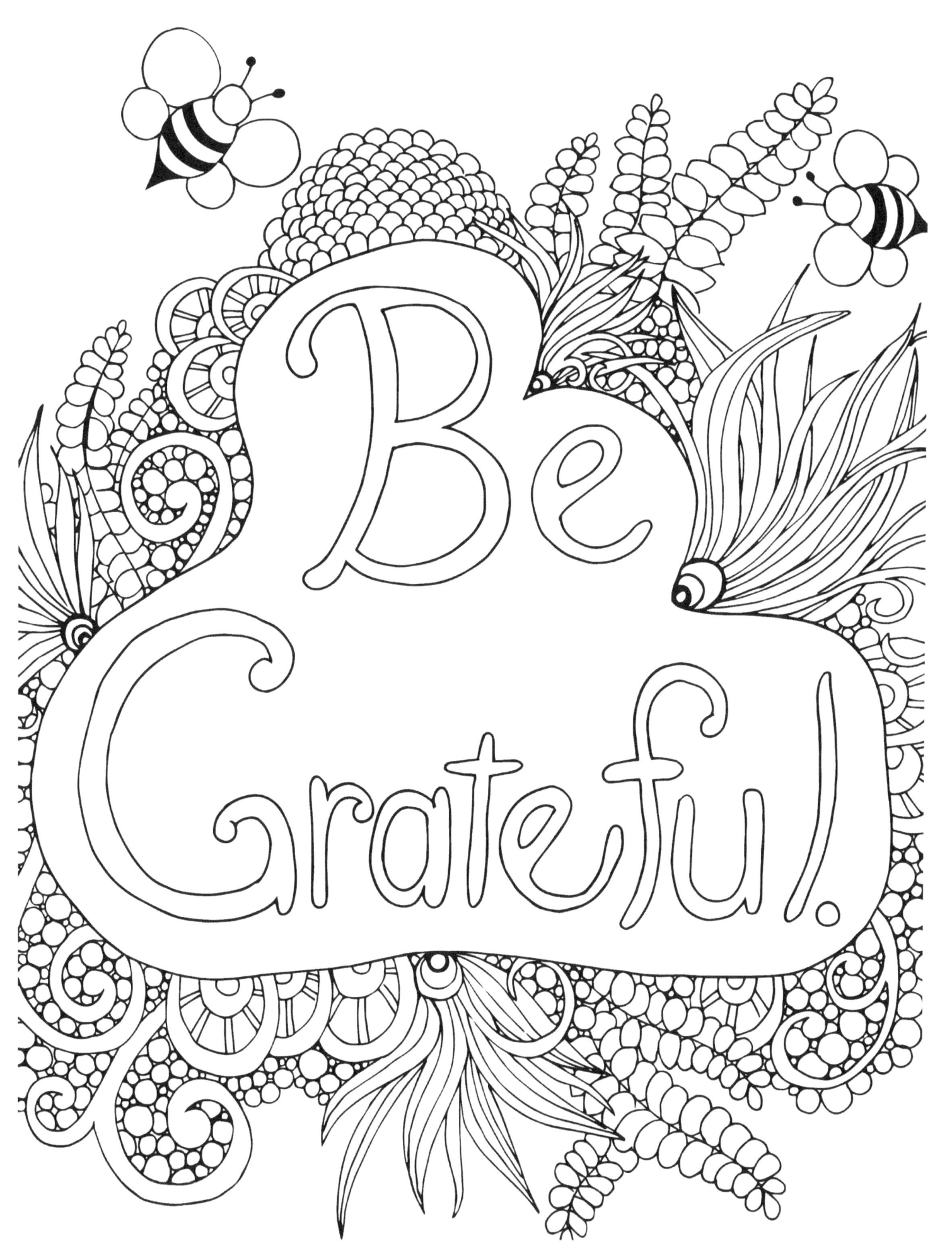

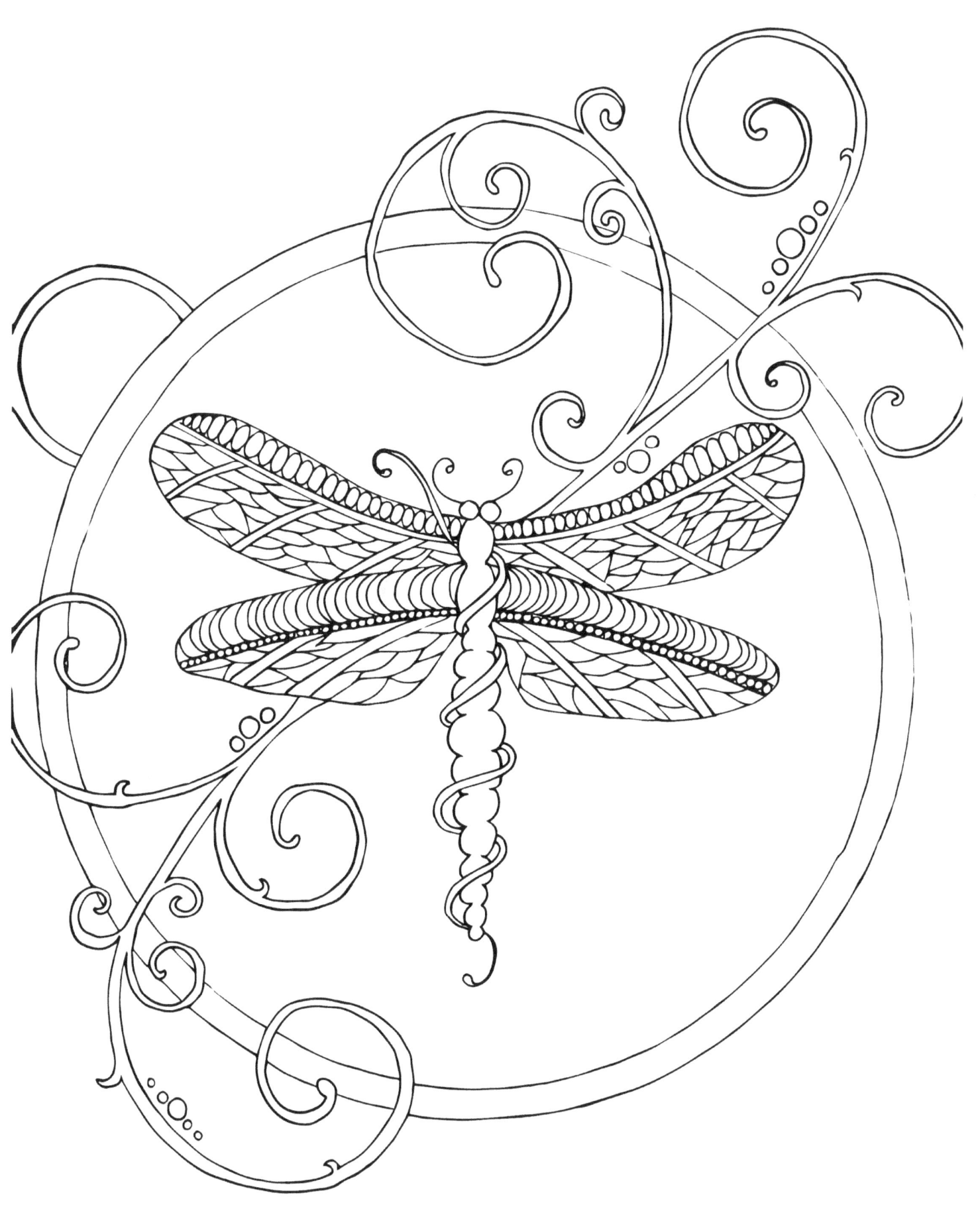

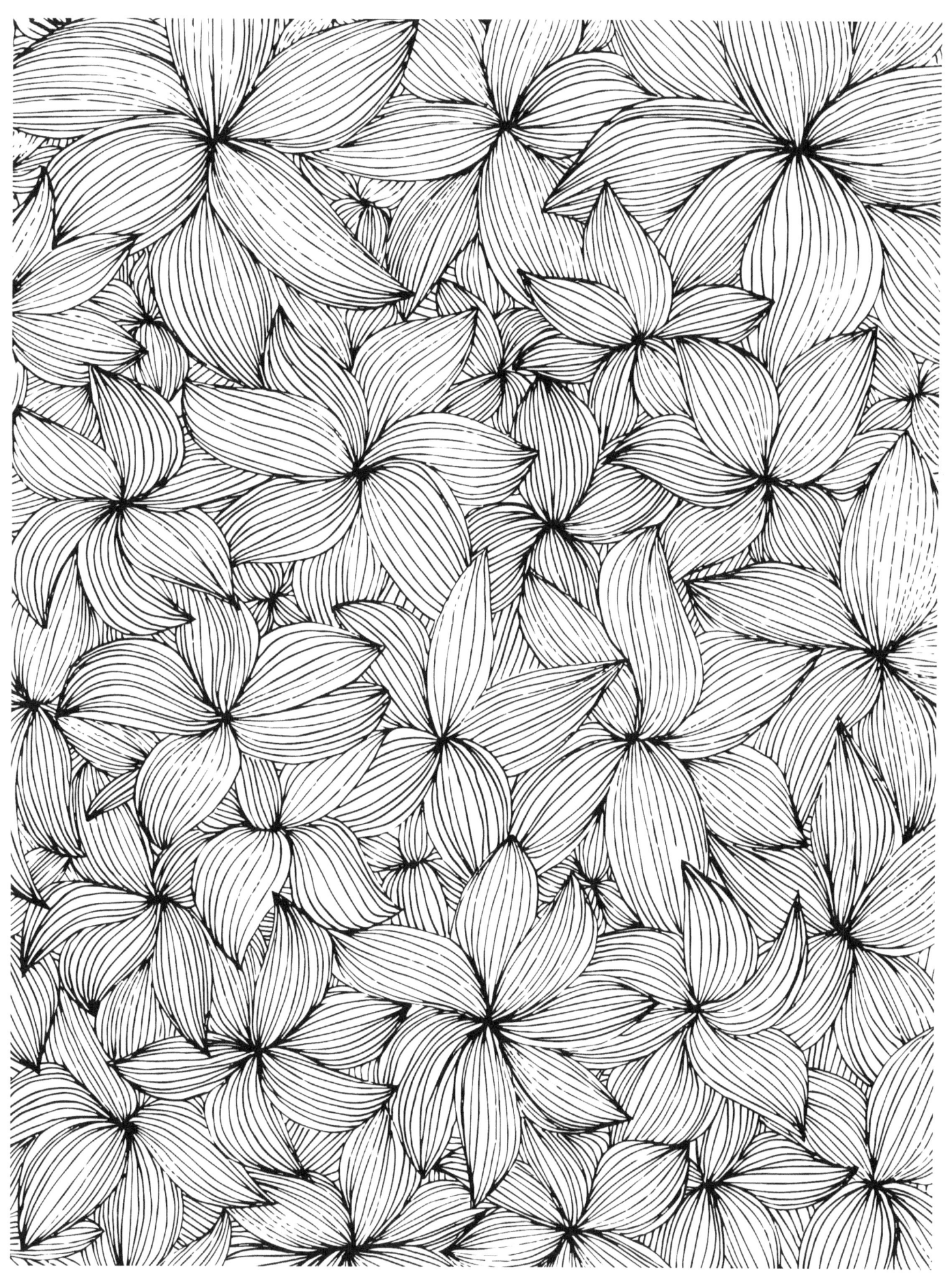

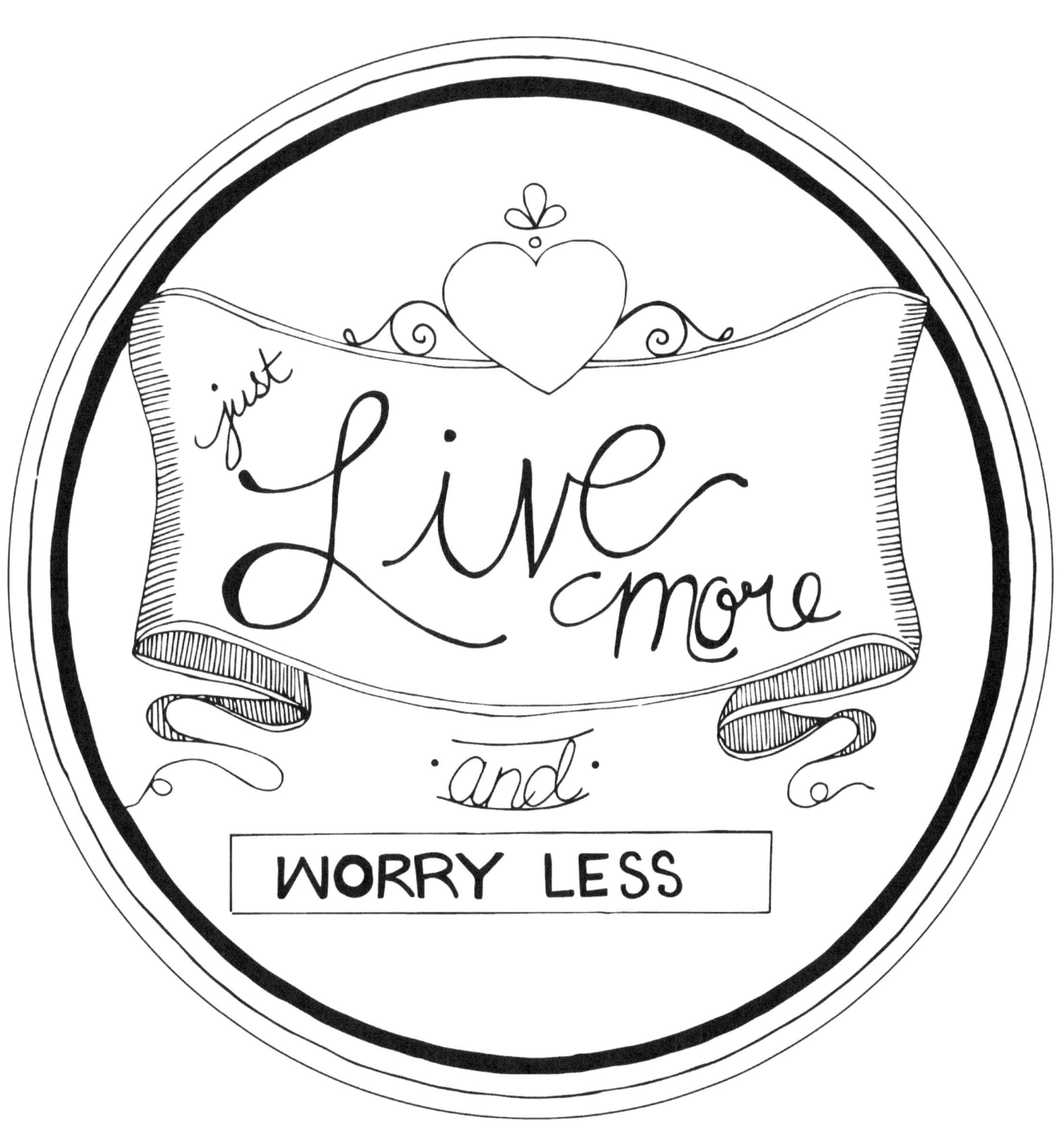

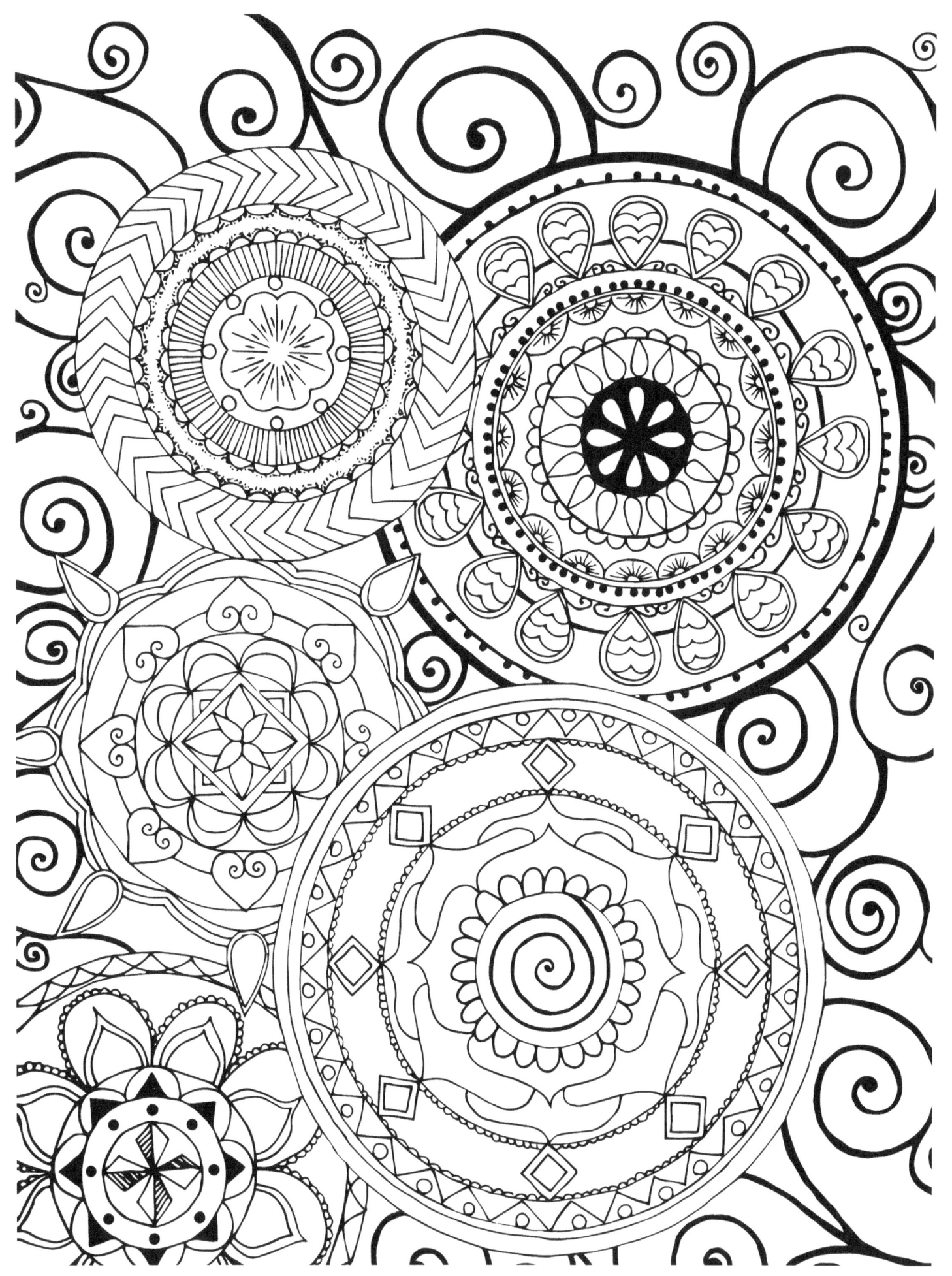

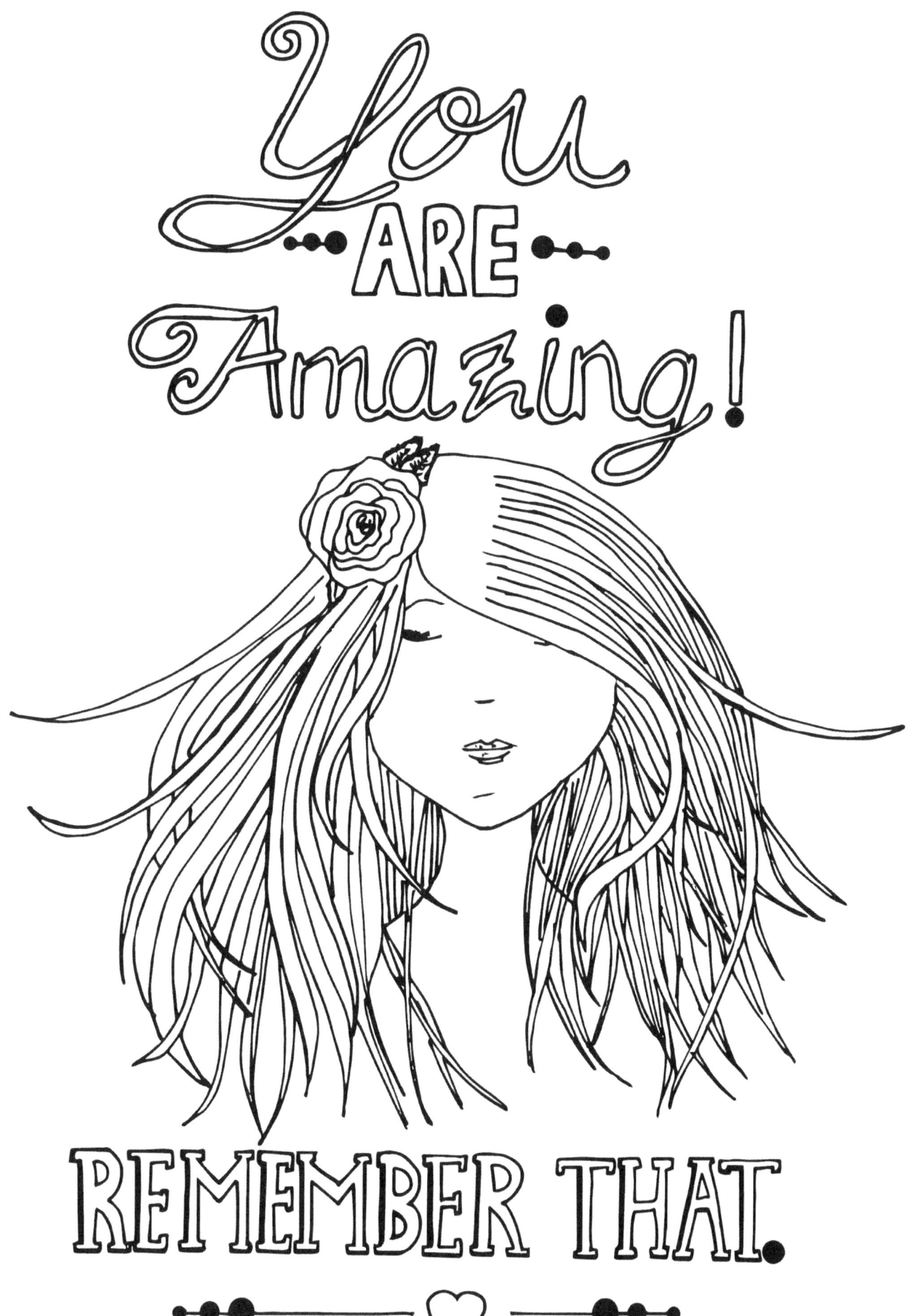

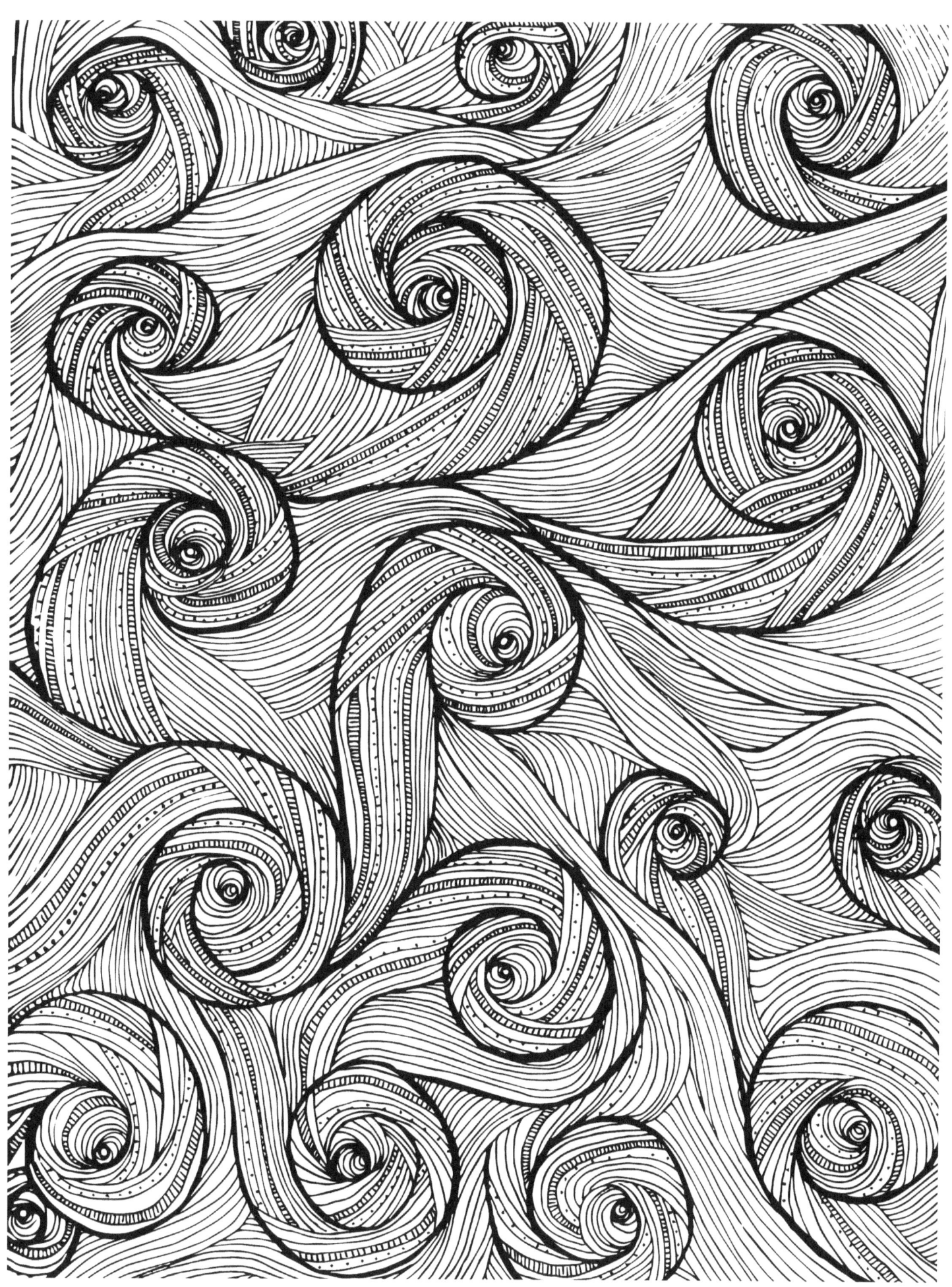

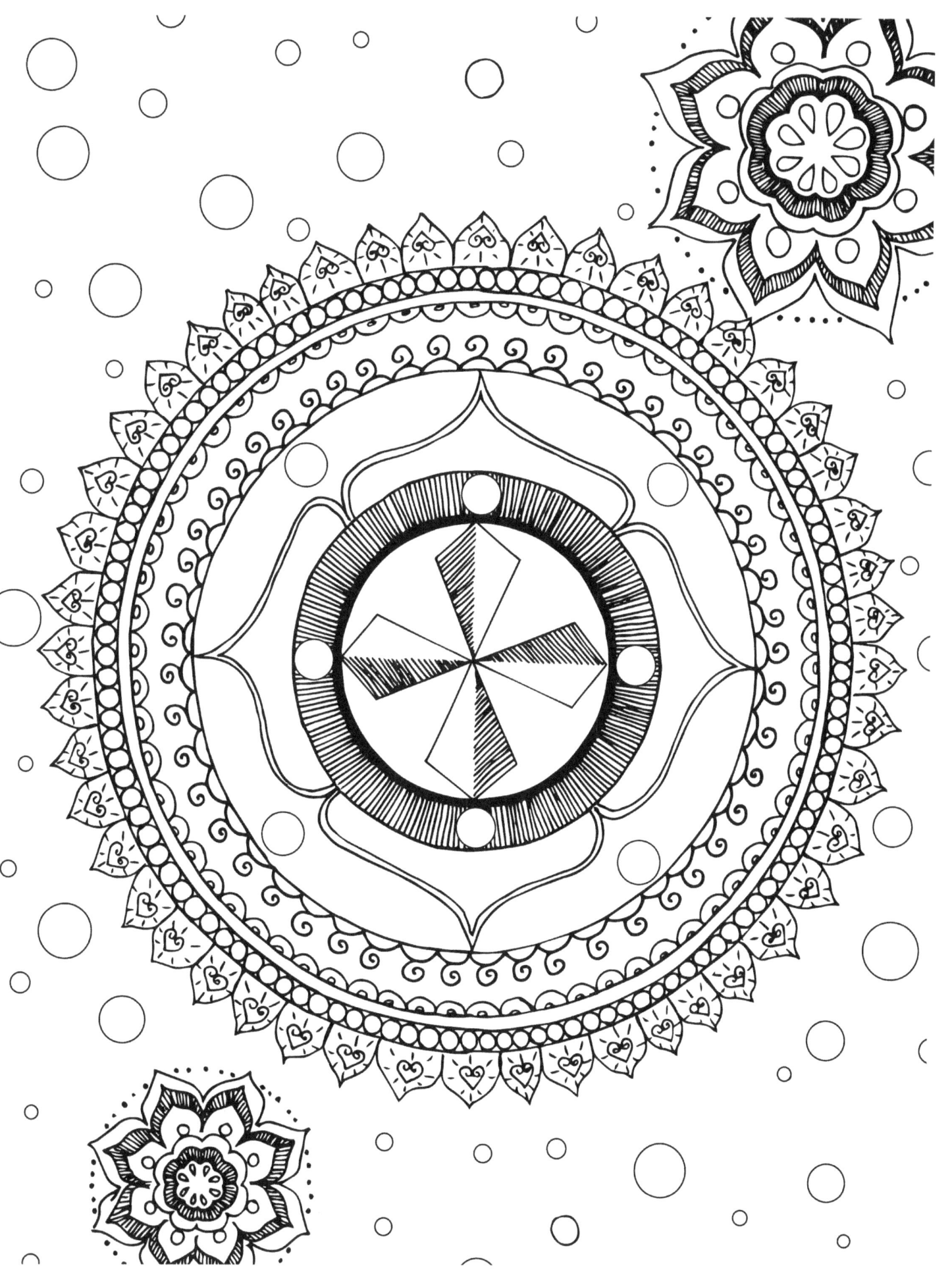

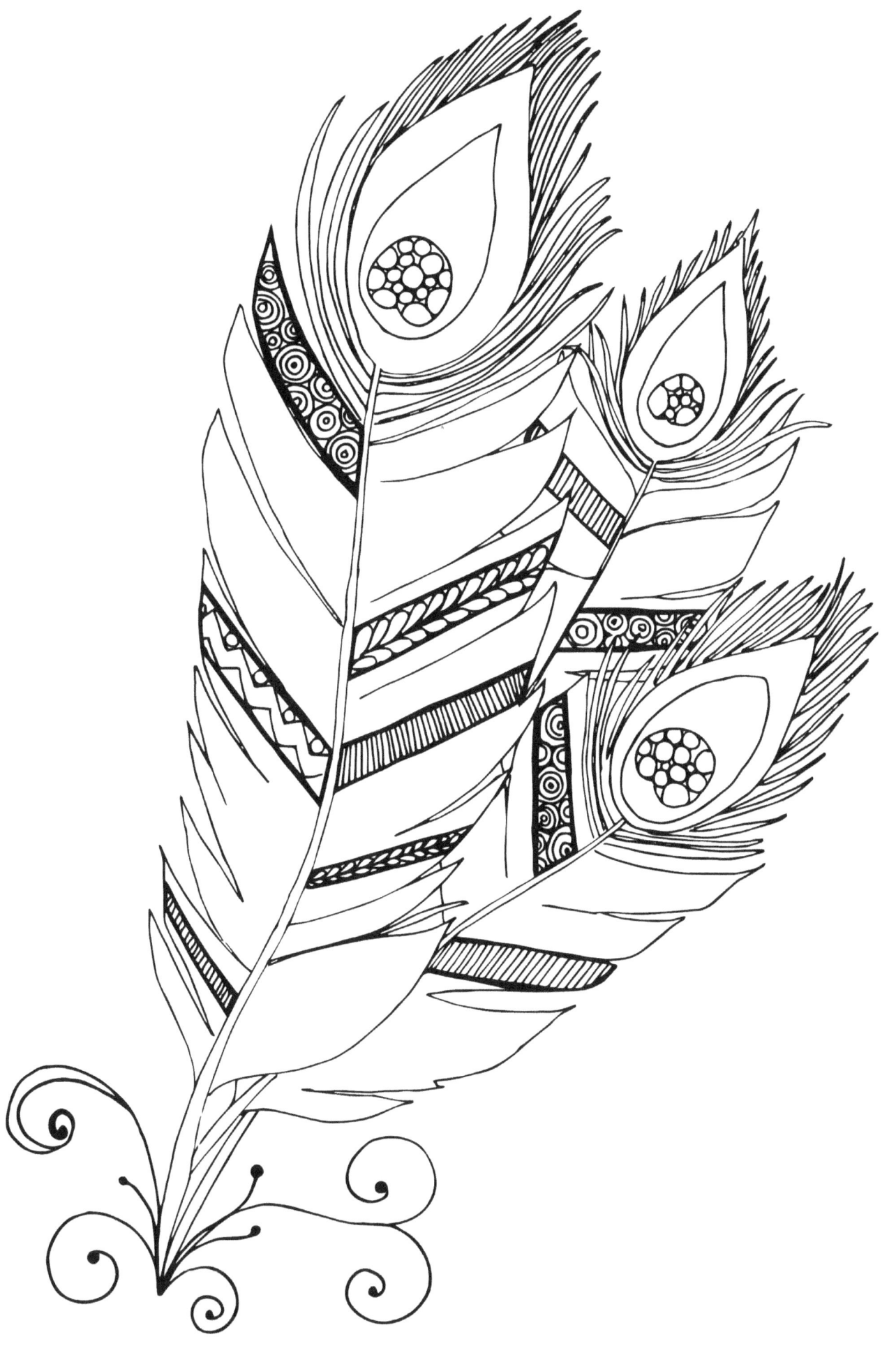

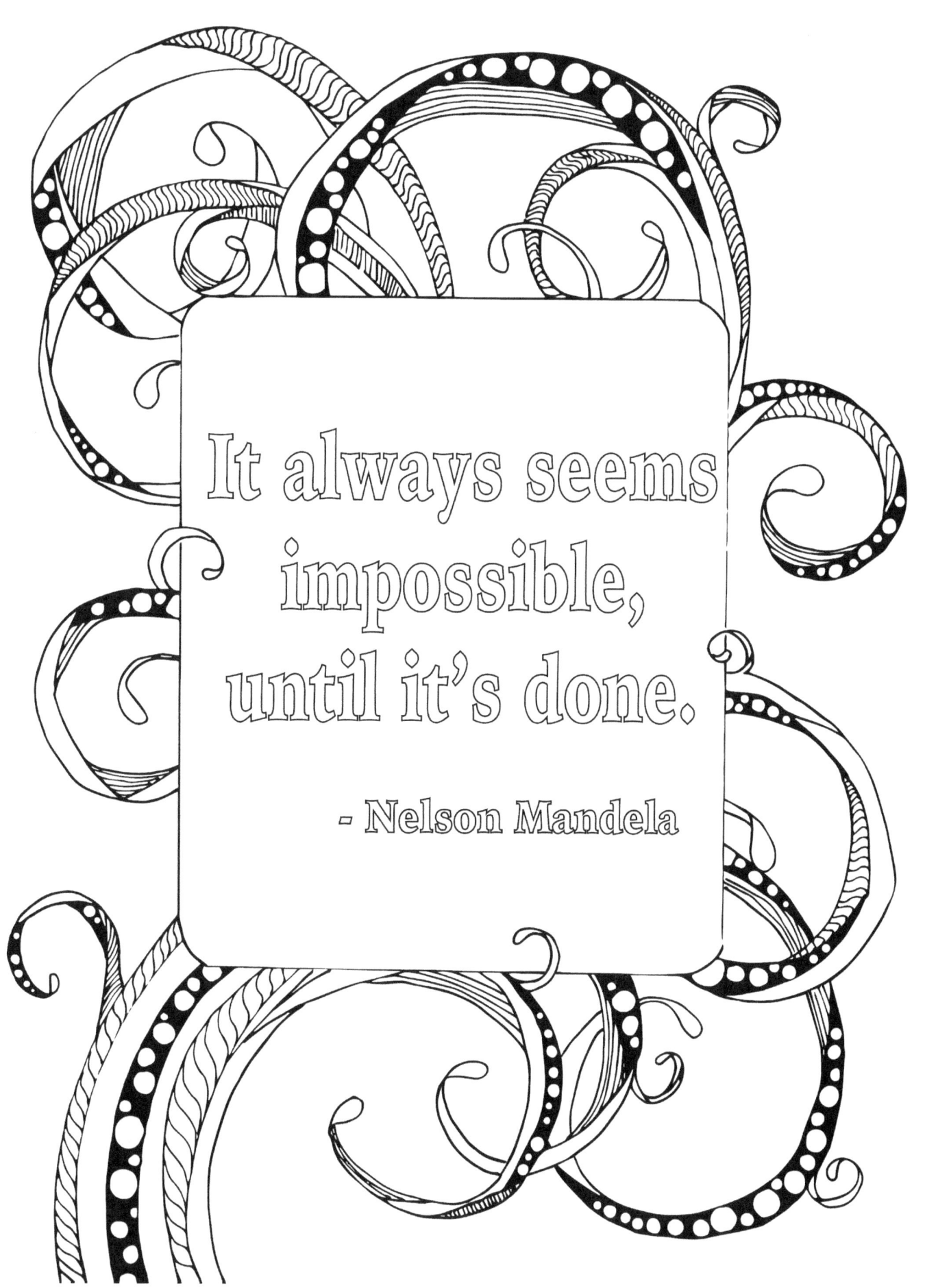

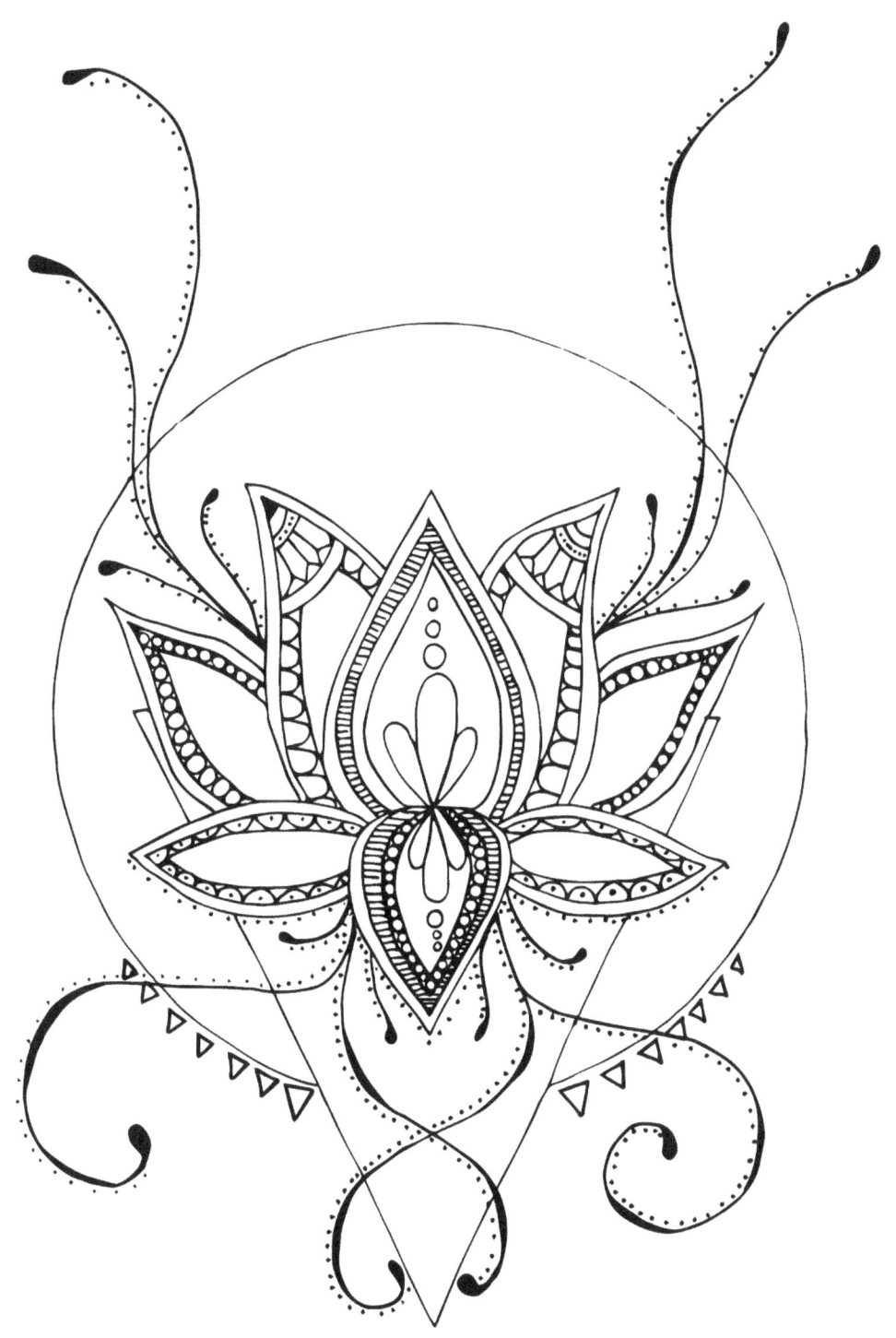

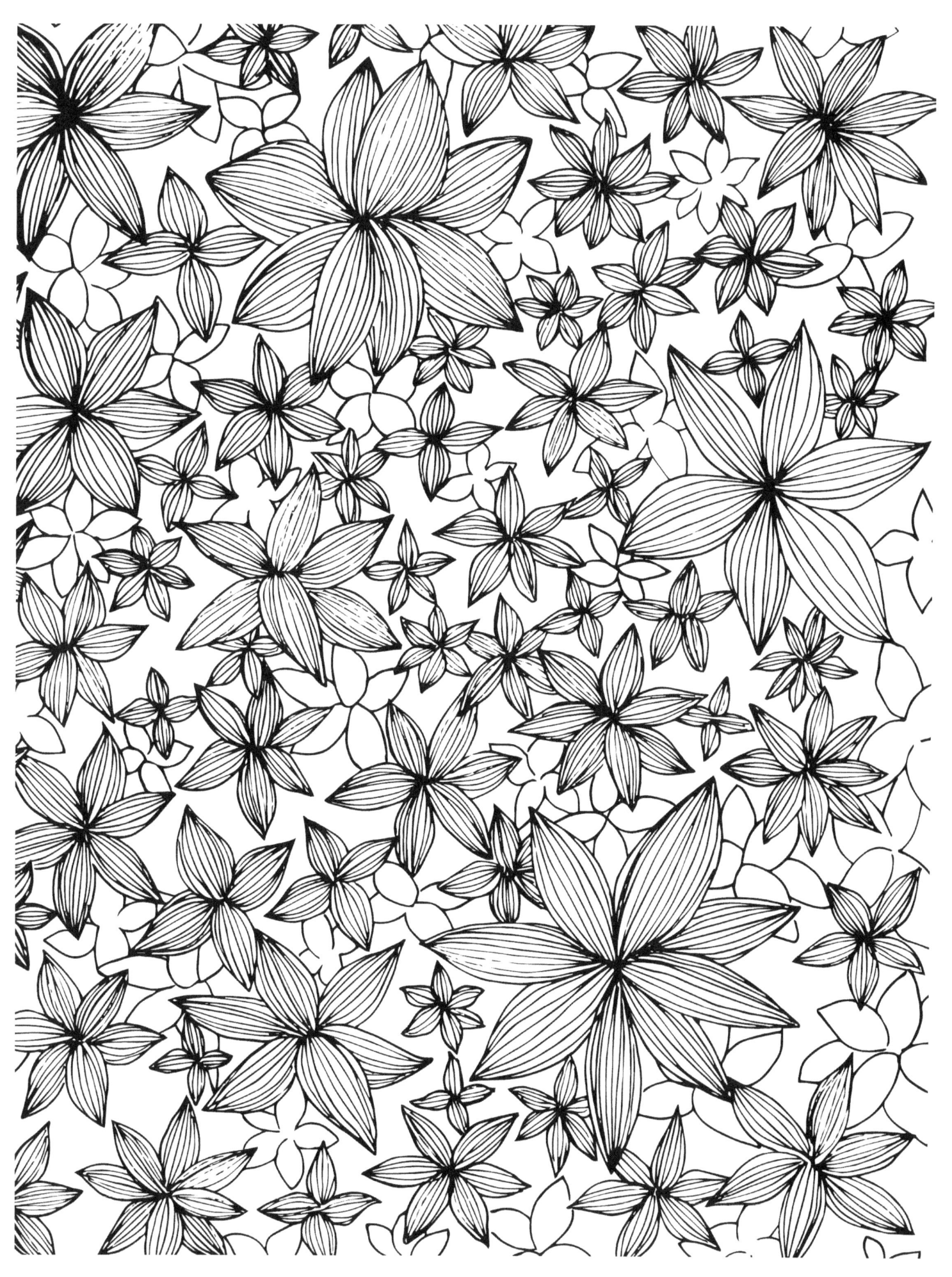

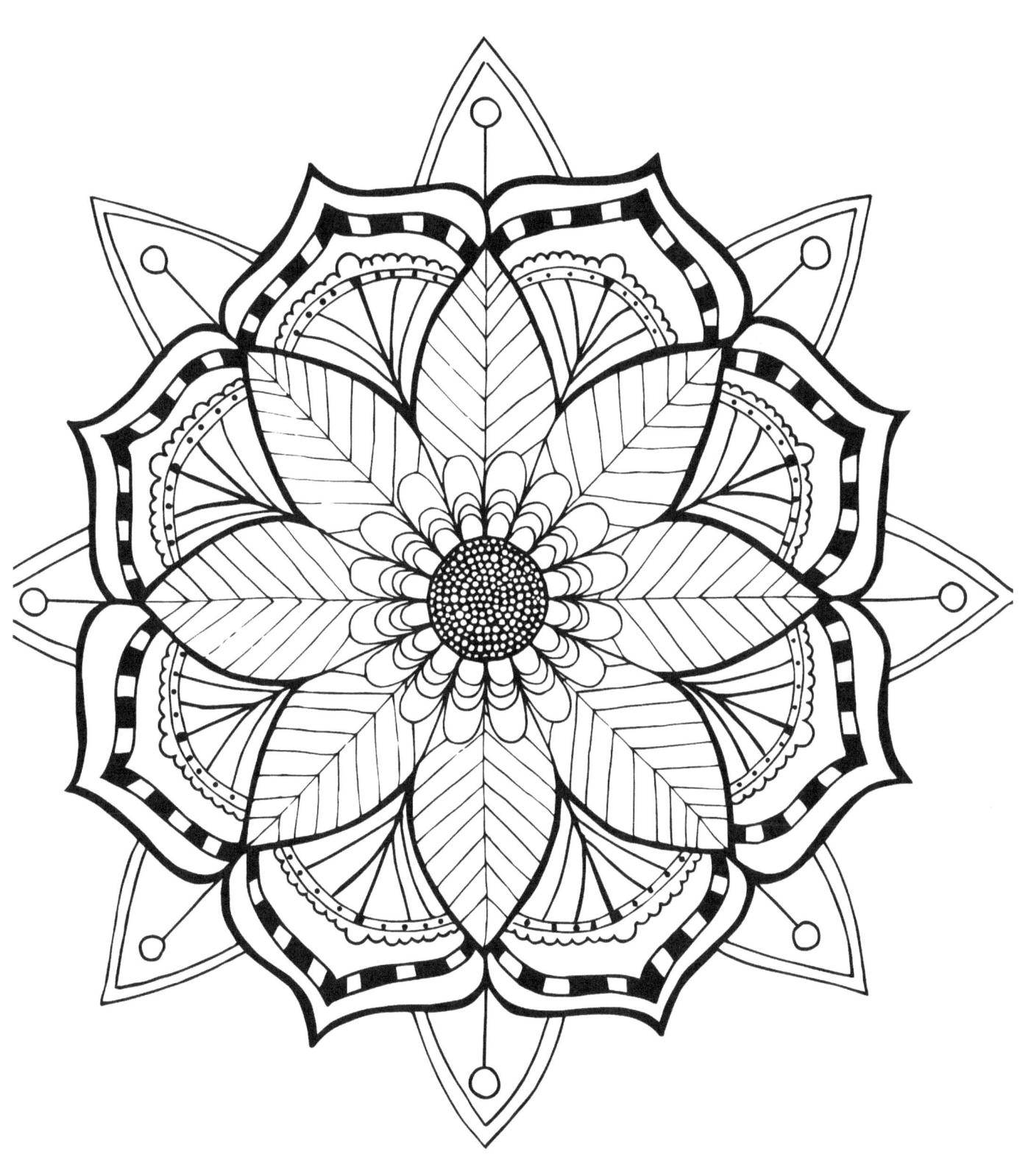

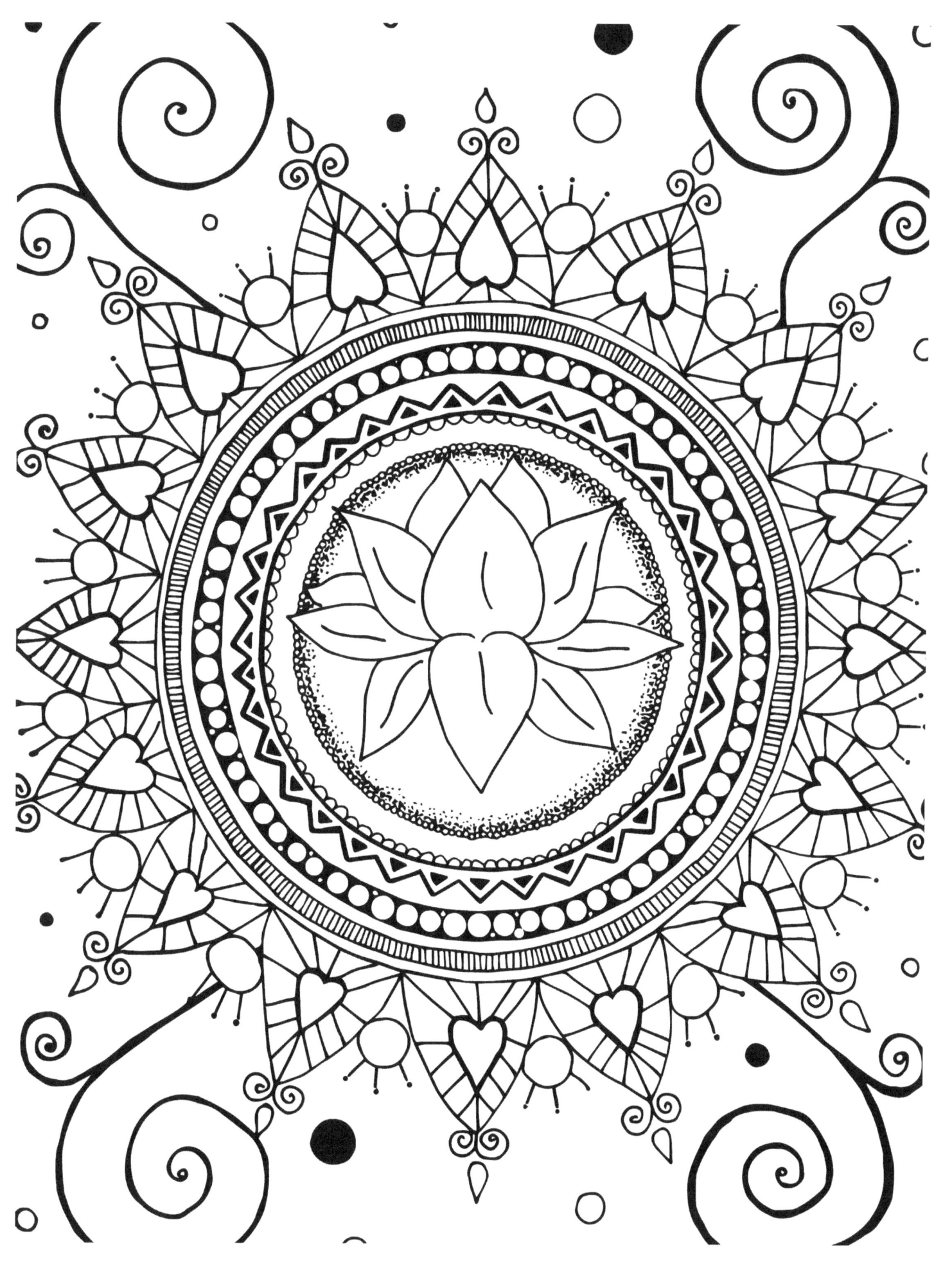

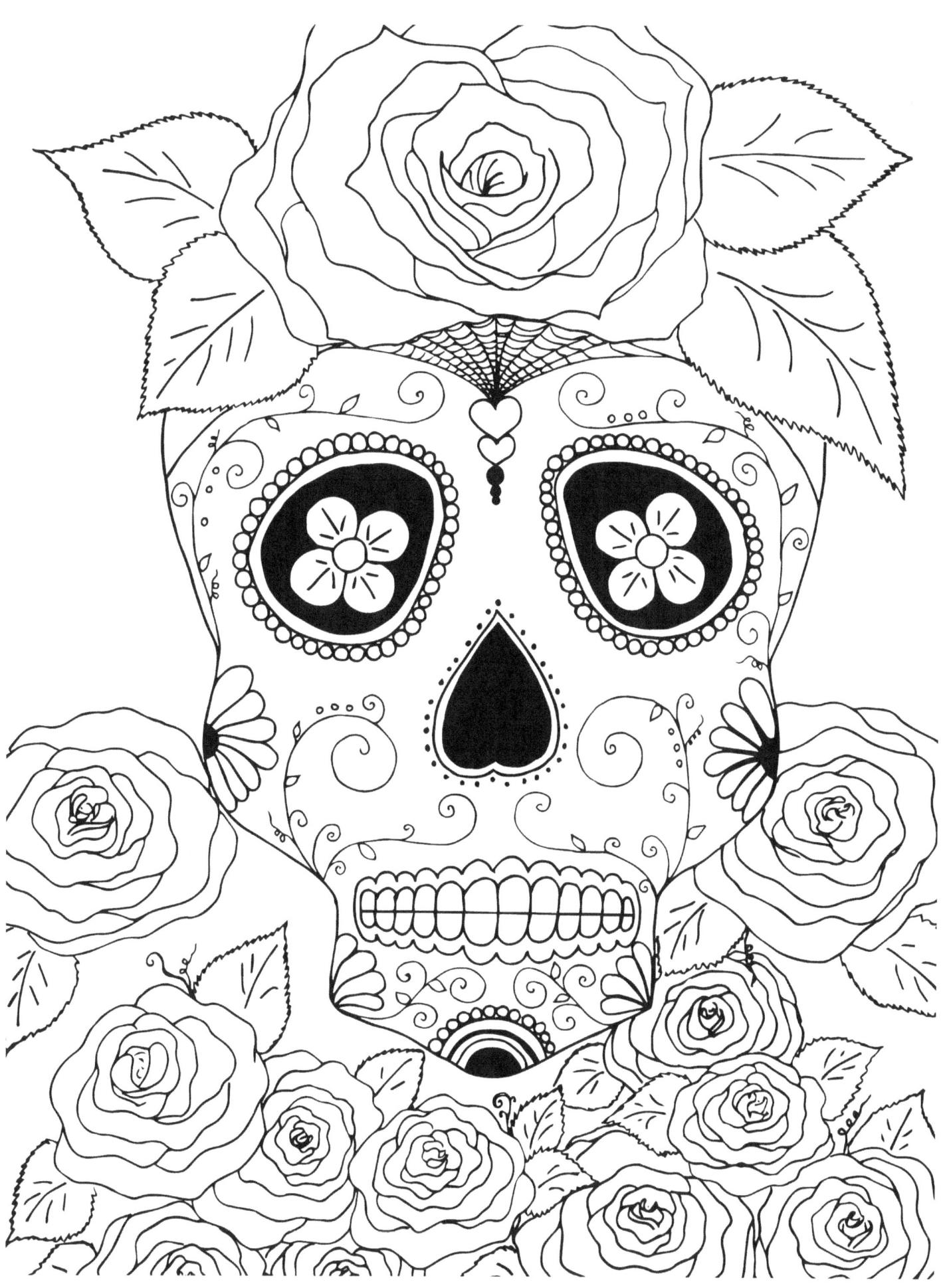

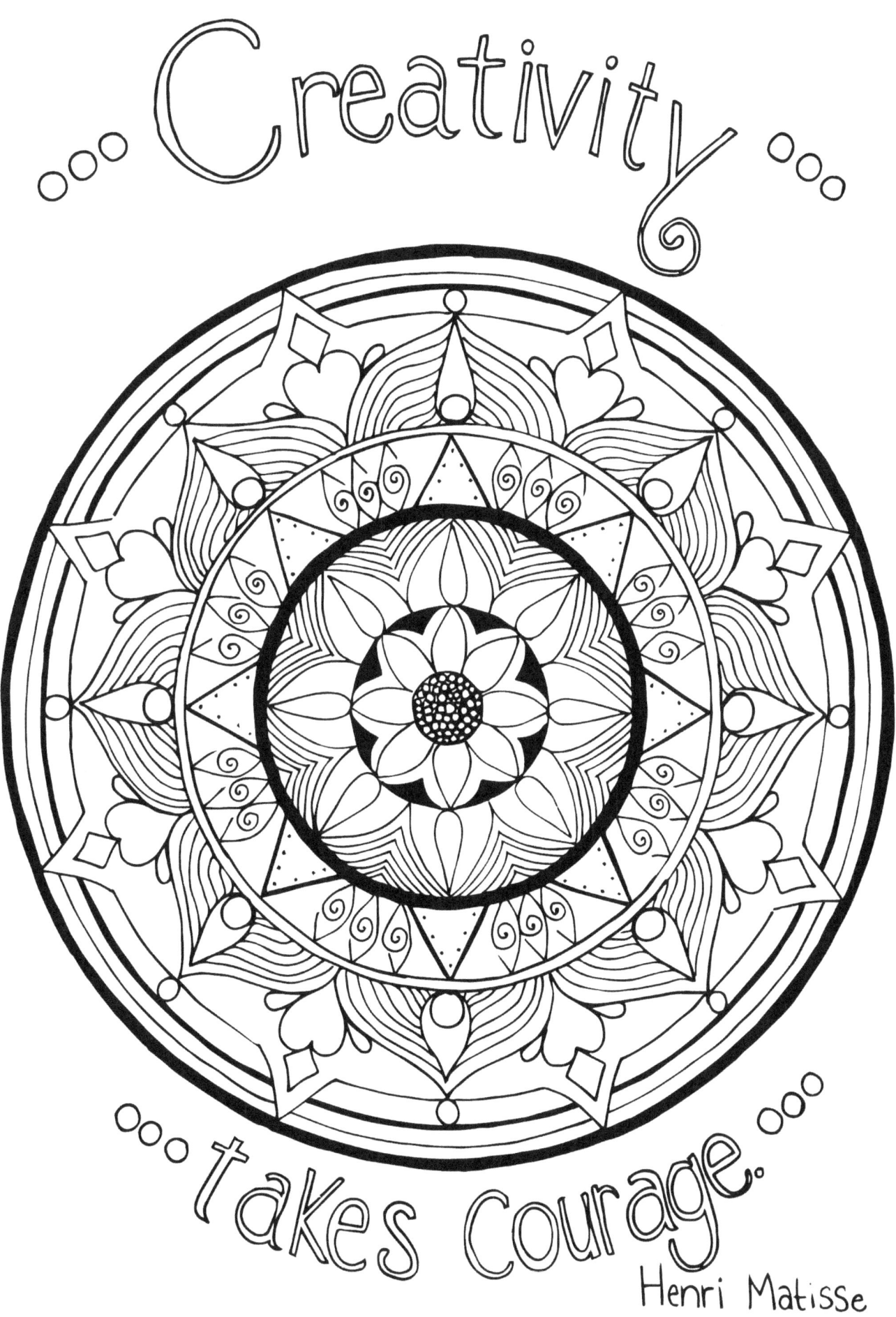

...Creativity...

...takes Courage...

Henri Matisse

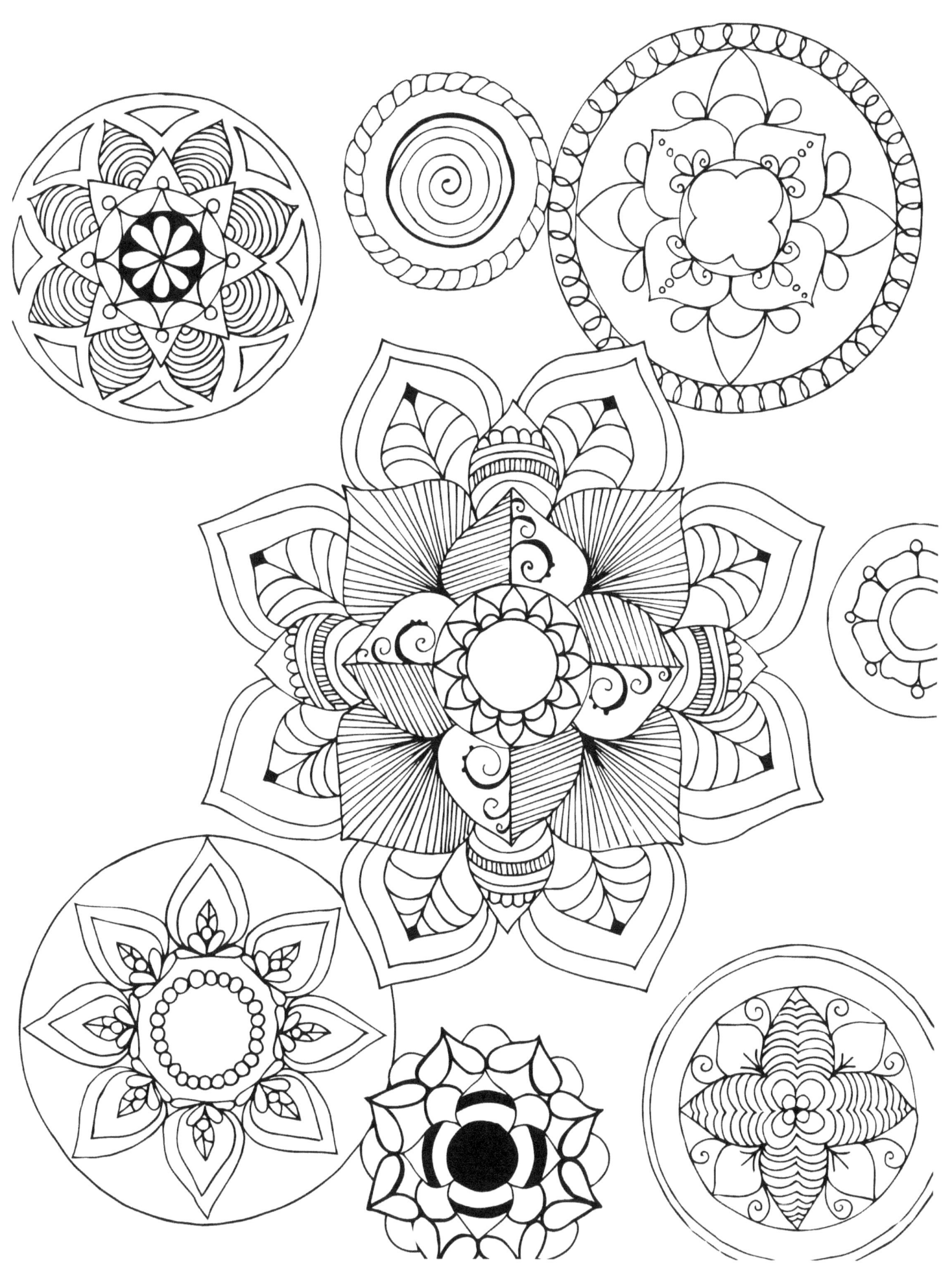

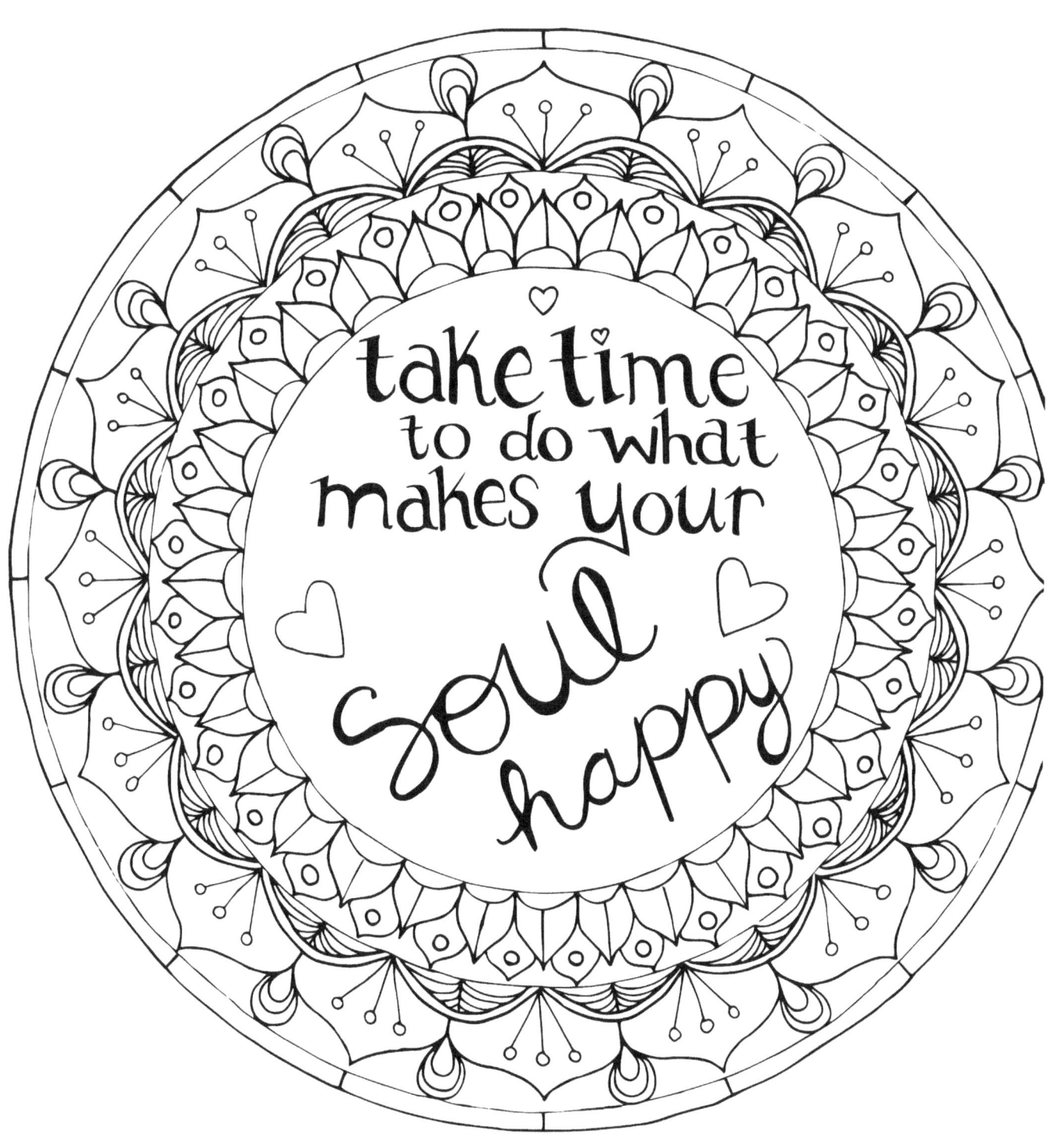

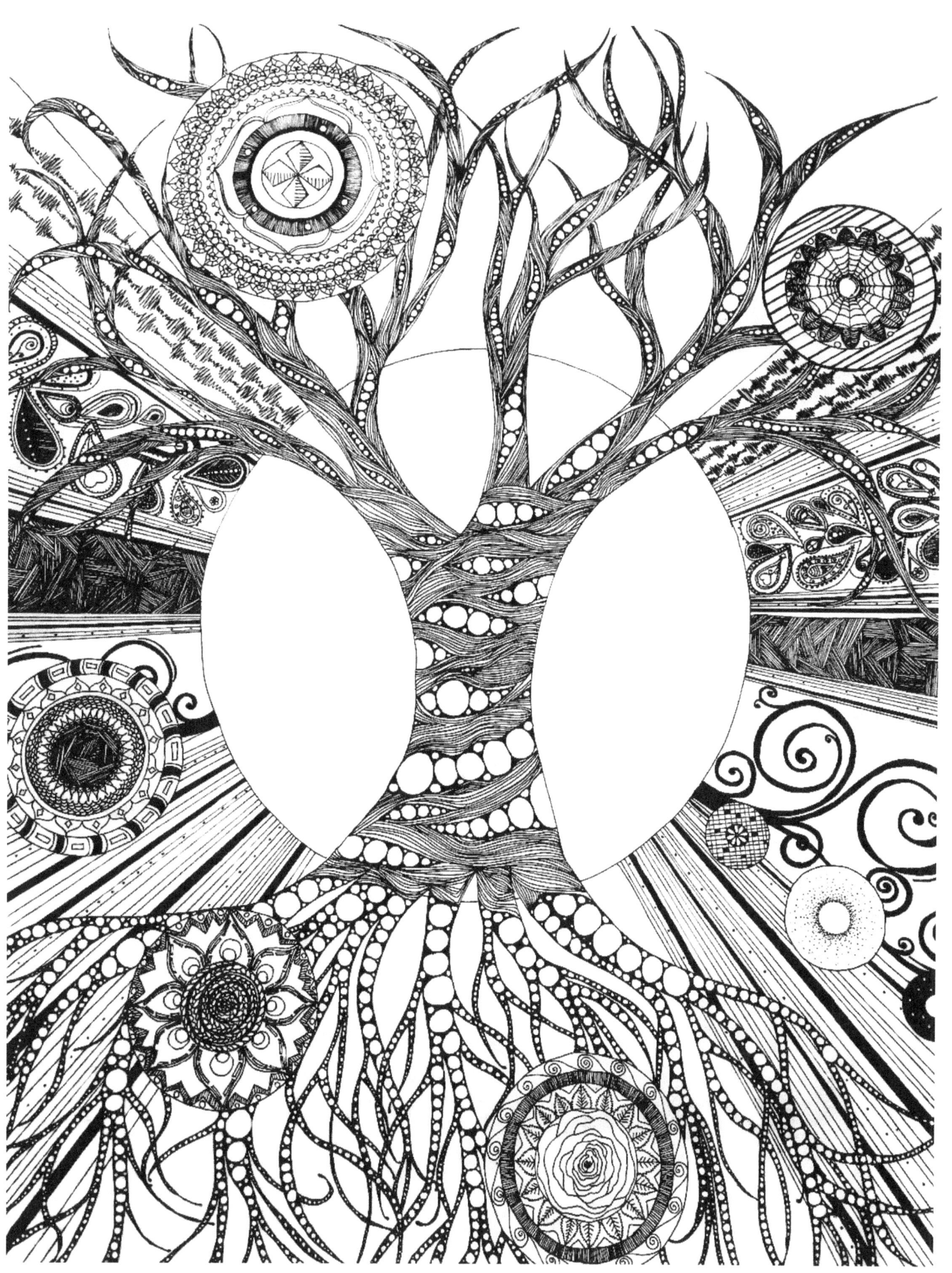

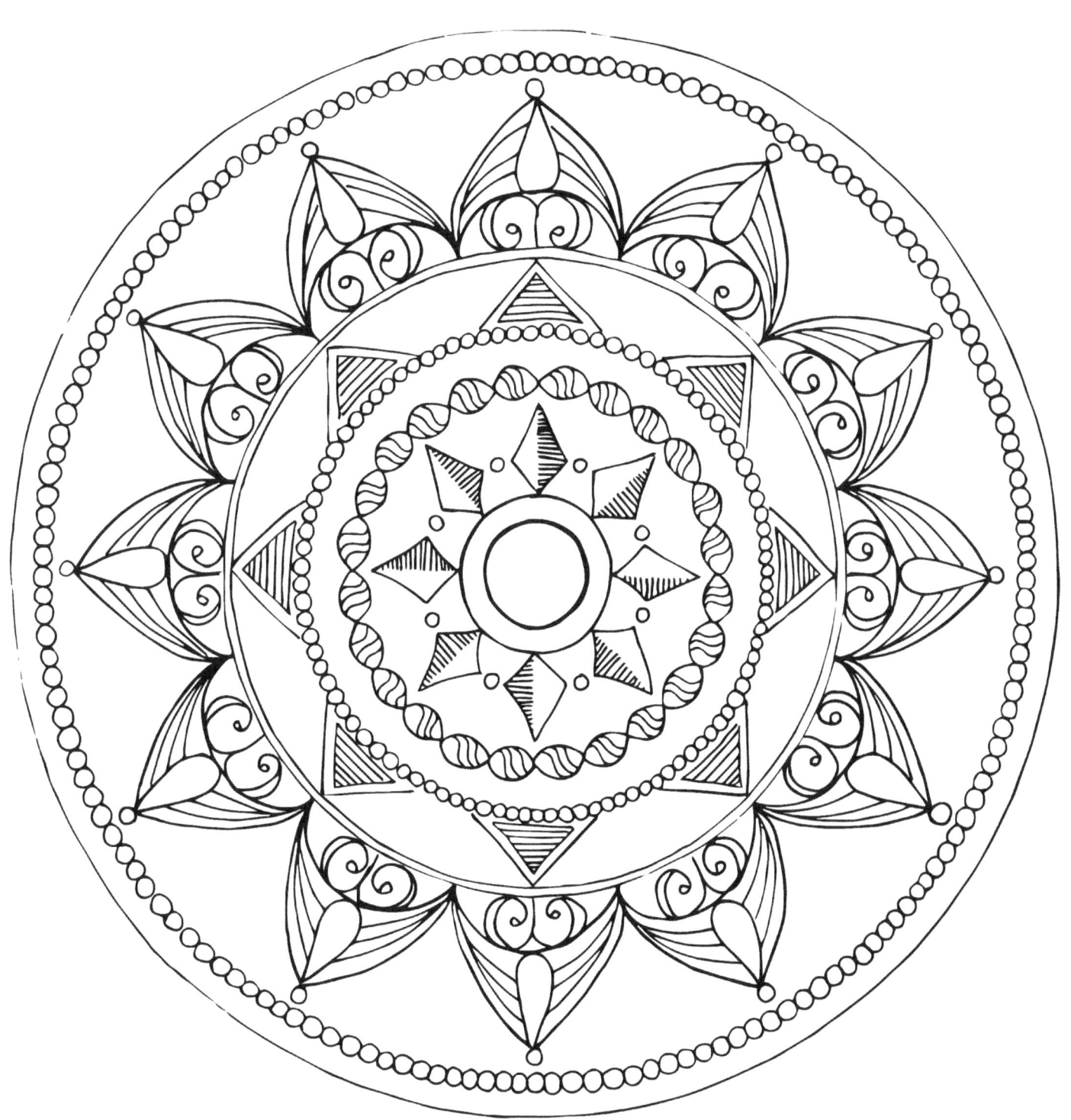

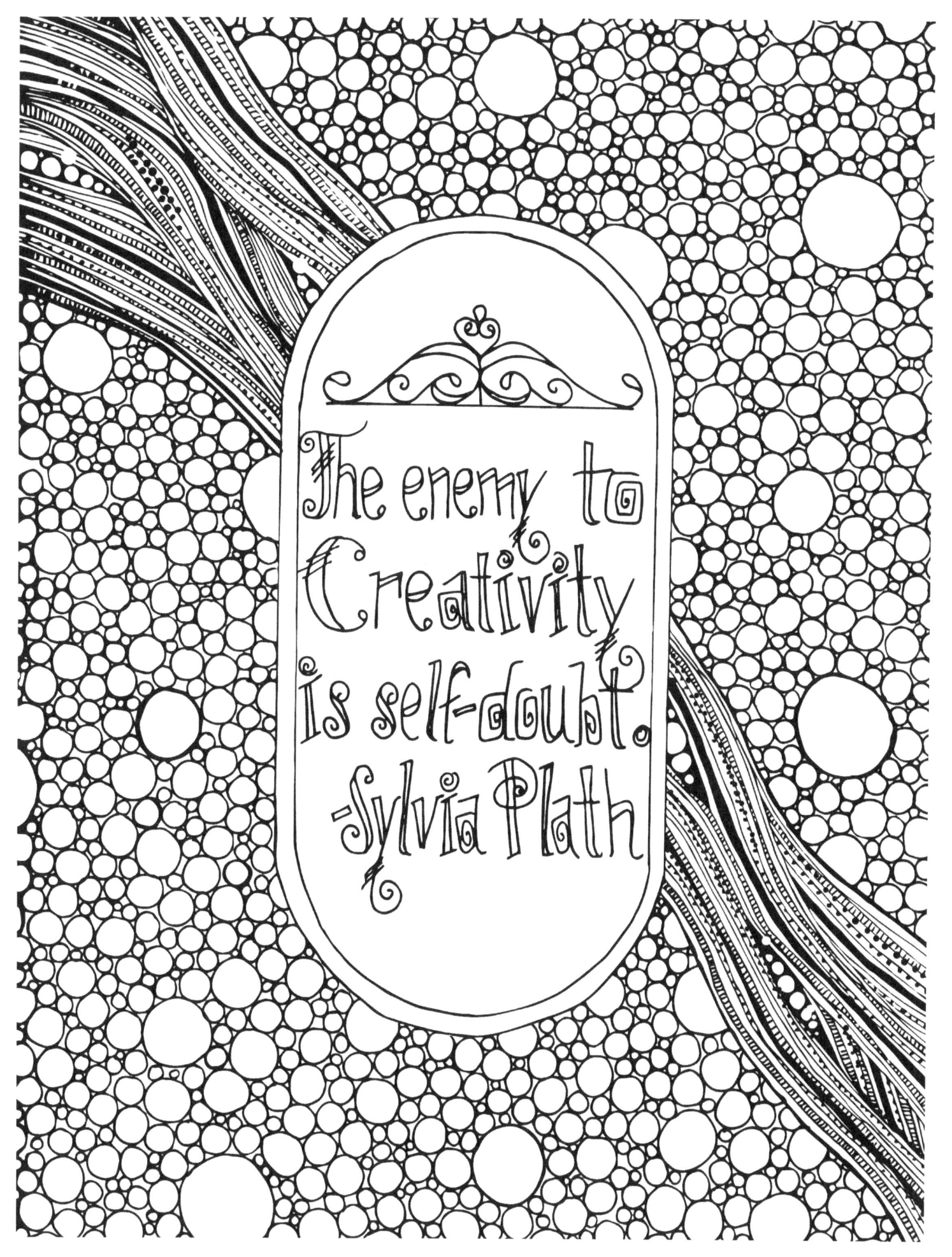

The enemy to Creativity is self-doubt.
-Sylvia Plath

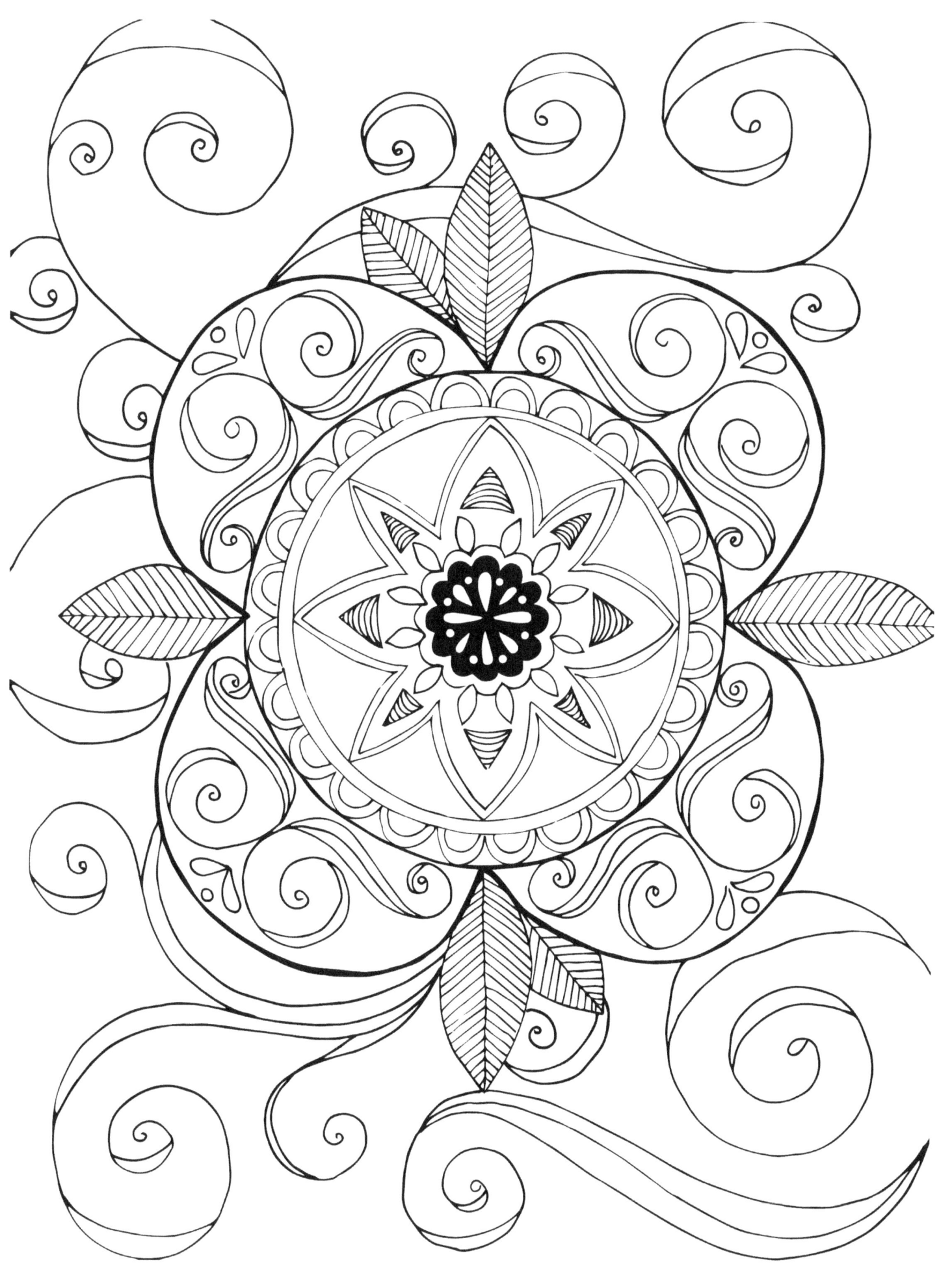

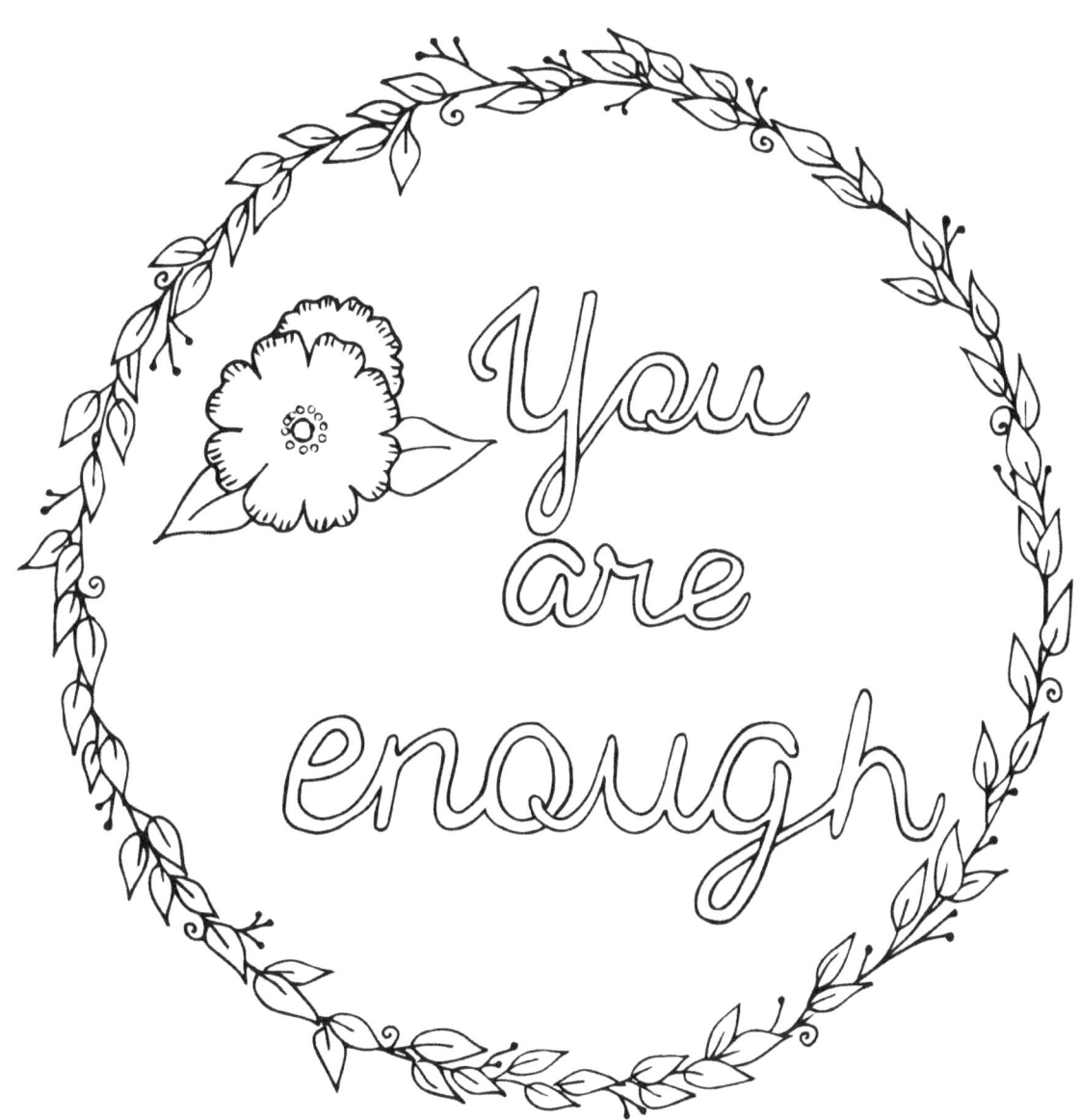

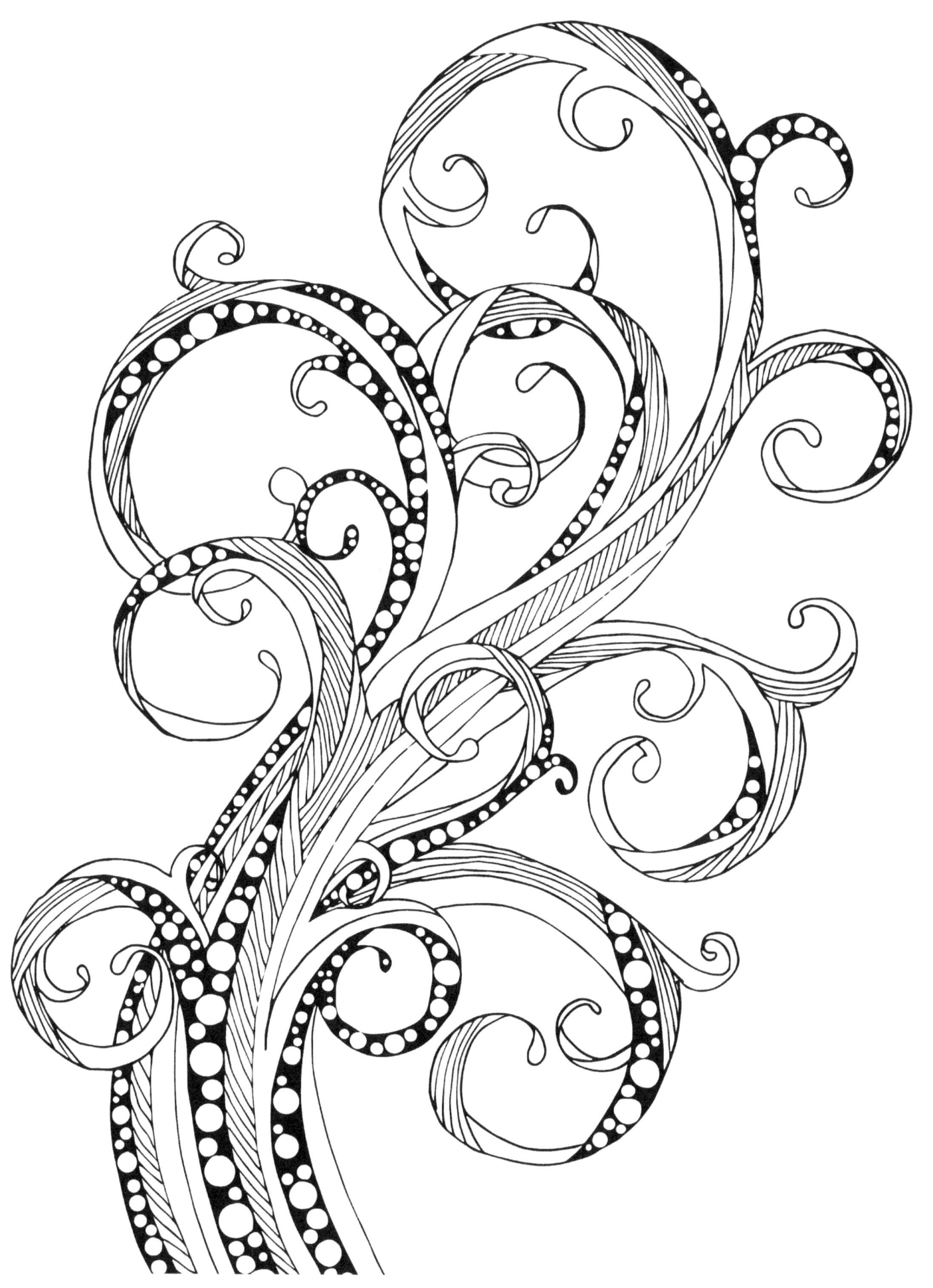

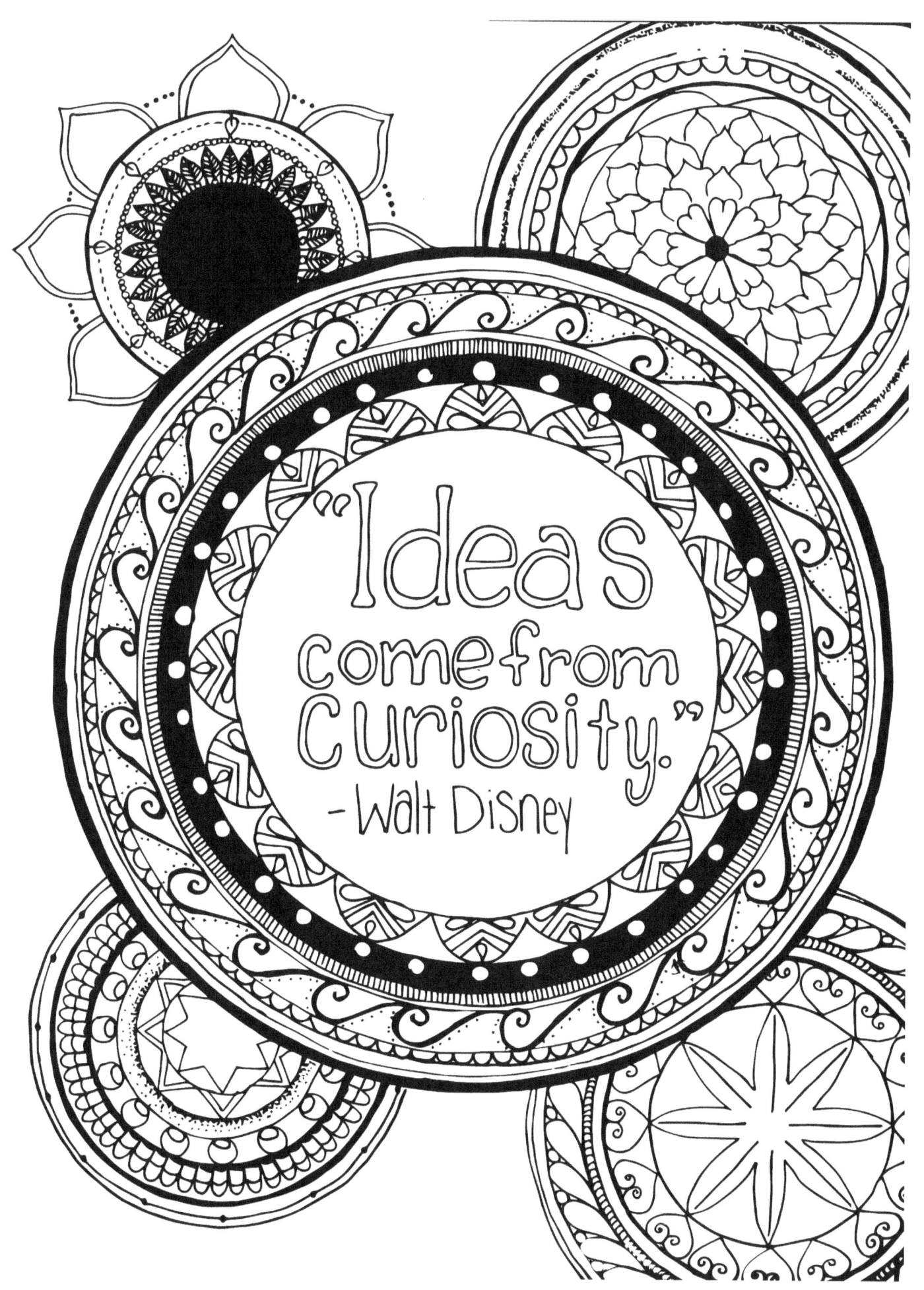

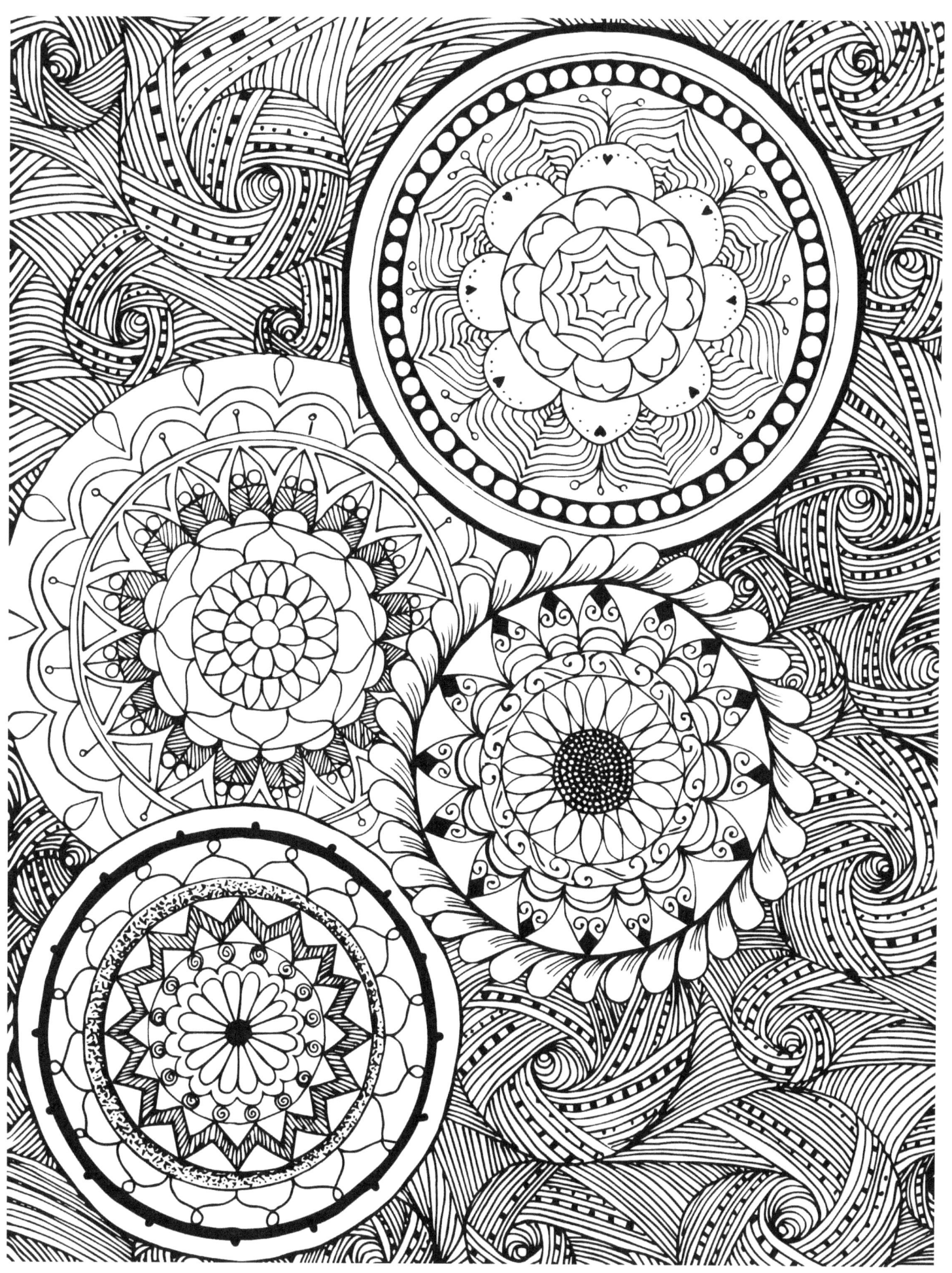

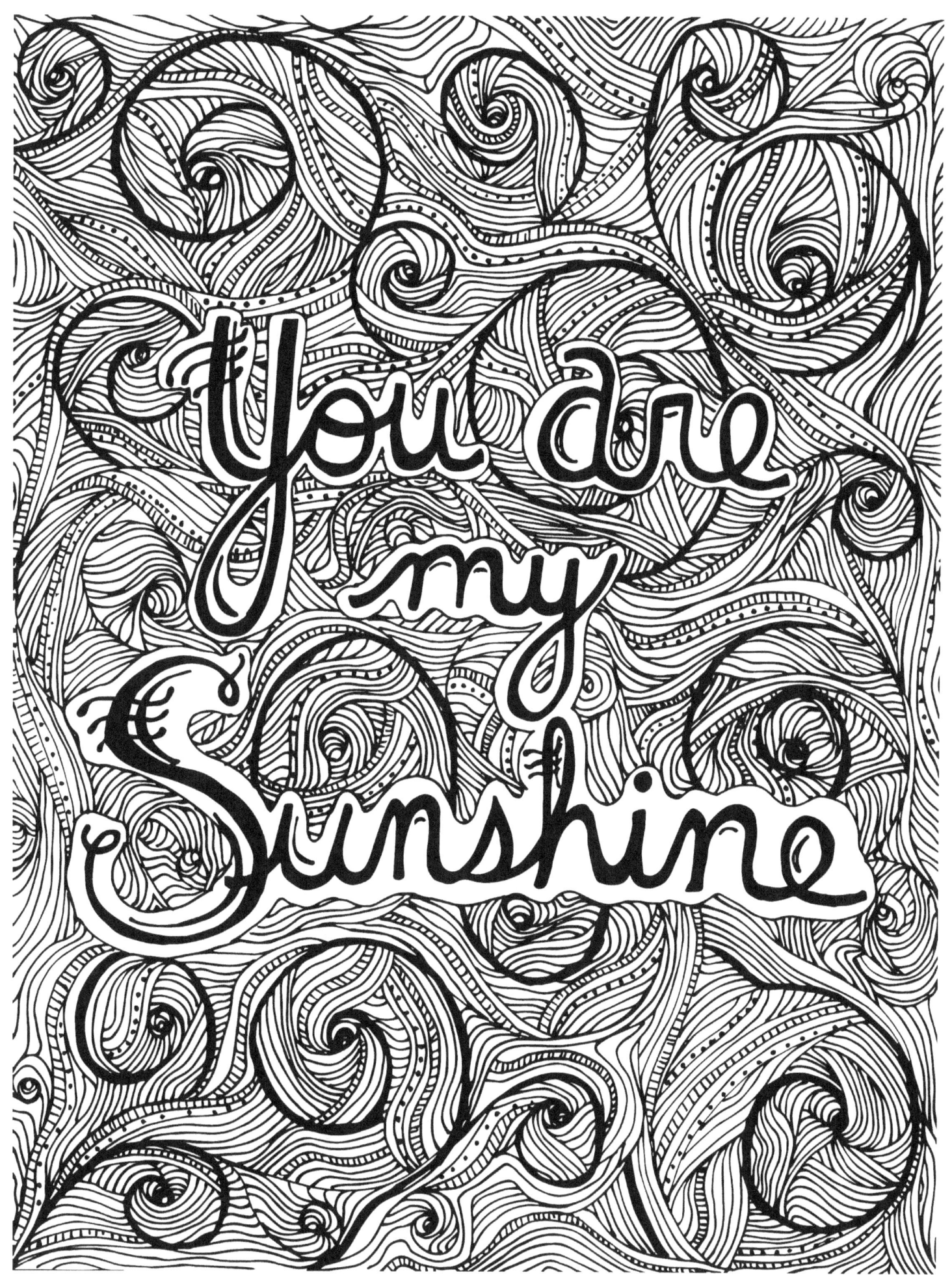

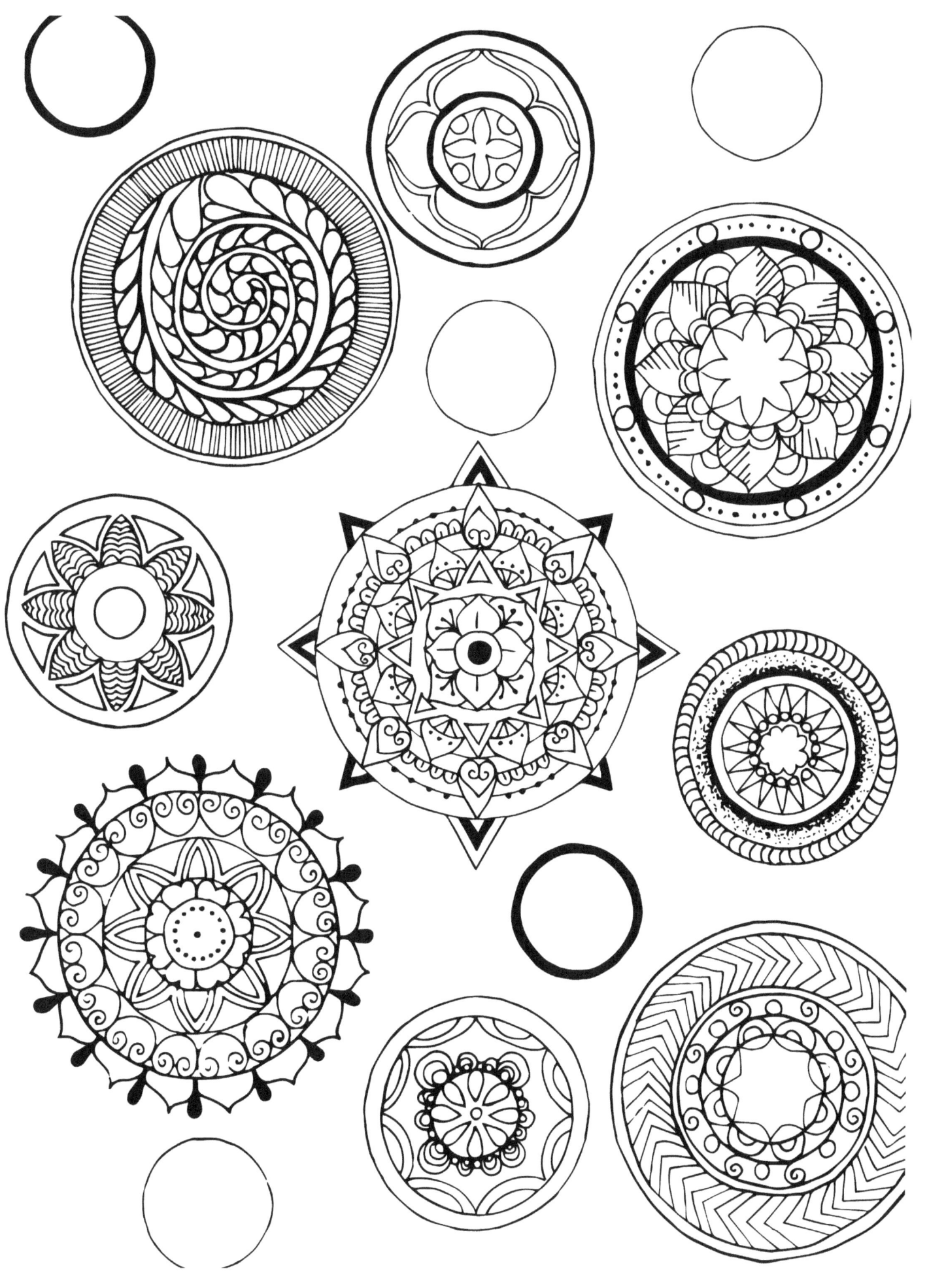

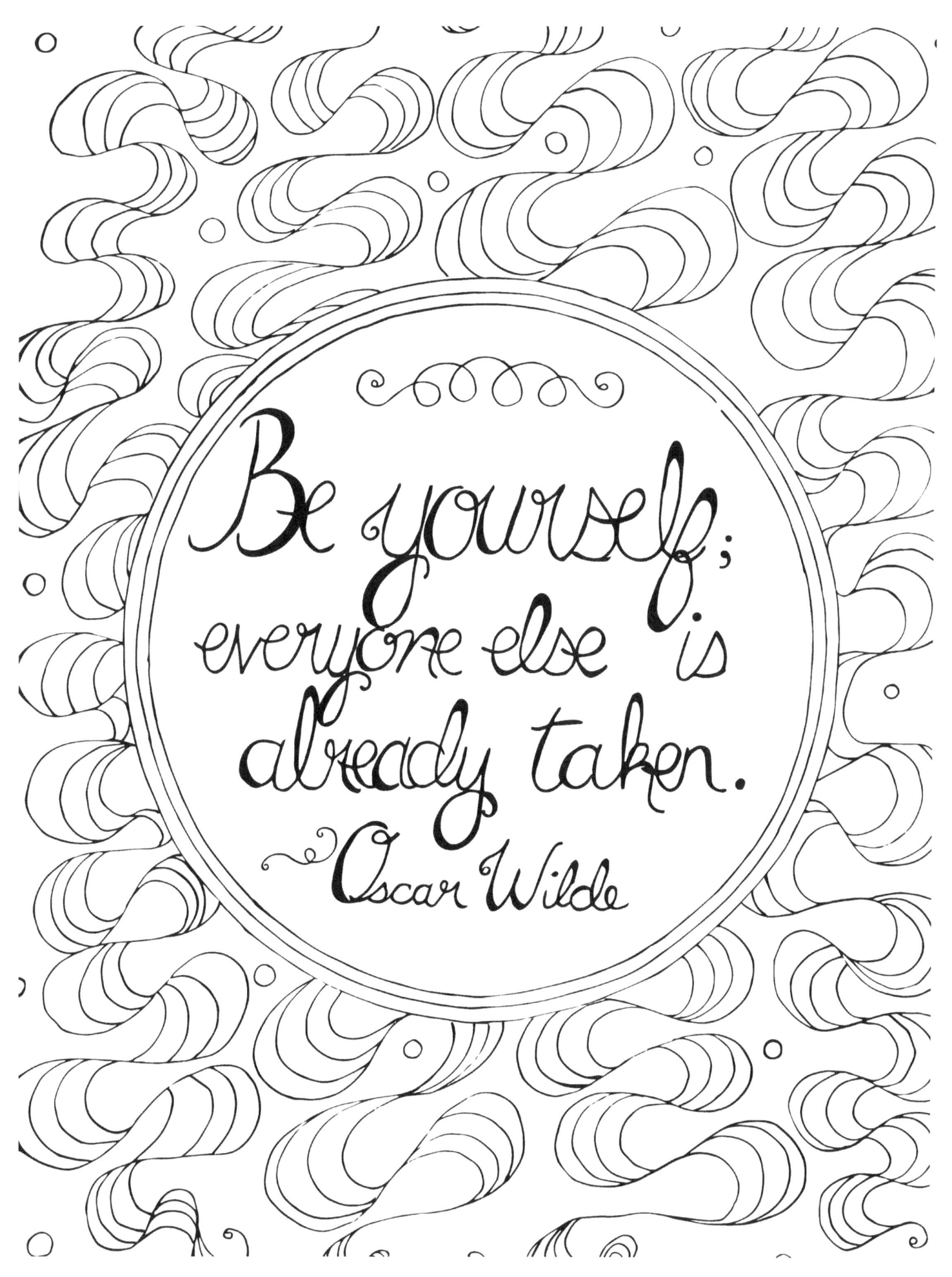

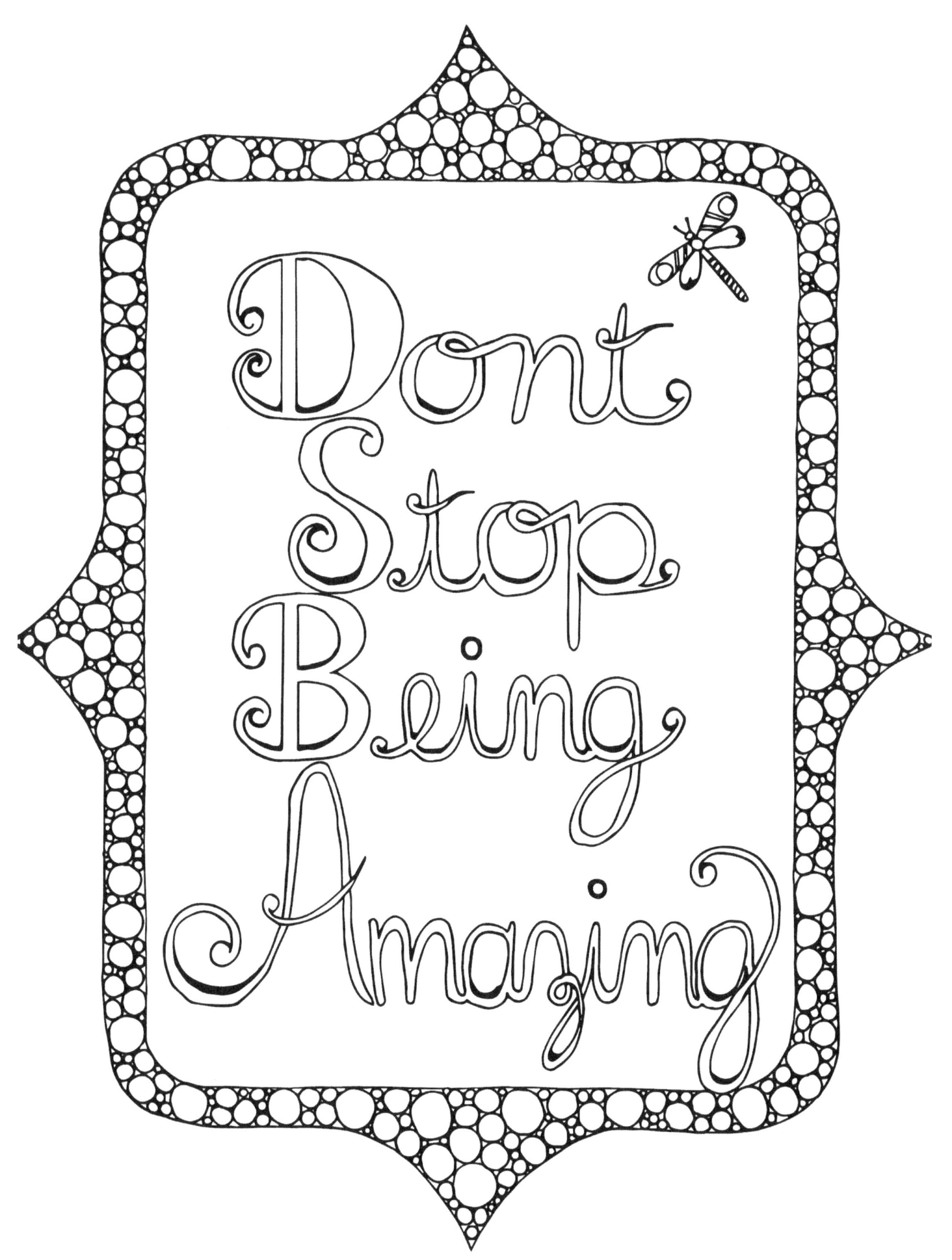